Build Your Business Vocabulary

John Flower

LTP
BUSINESS

Language Teaching Publications
114a Church Rd, Hove, BN3 2EB, England

© Language Teaching Publications 1990
ISBN 0 906717 87 6
Reprinted 1990, 91, 92, 94 (twice), 95, 96, 98, 2000

NO UNAUTHORISED PHOTOCOPYING

Acknowledgements

Cover design by Anna Macleod.
Cover photograph courtesy of Zefa.
Many thanks to Michael Lewis for his encouragement and guidance, and to James Slater for his drawings.

I am also grateful to my colleagues and students for all their help, and to Ruth, Helen and Andrew for putting up with it all.

Building your business vocabulary efficiently

So you plan to build your vocabulary! Learning vocabulary is a very important part of learning English. If you make a grammar mistake, it may be "wrong" but very often people will understand you anyway. But if you don't know the exact word that you need, it is very frustrating for you, and the person you are talking to. Good business English means having a big vocabulary!

There are better and worse ways to build your vocabulary and this book will help you to build your vocabulary quickly and effectively.

You will find it is best to work:

- systematically
- regularly
- personally

Don't just make lists of all the new words you meet – plan and choose. Think of areas **you** are interested in; look for things **you** can't say in English, then fill those gaps in **your** vocabulary.

Think abut the kind of vocabulary you need. What about social English? The language of business letters? Reading in special areas such as public relations or international trade? Building your business vocabulary is a big job – you can help yourself by choosing the things that are most use to you and learning those first.

You can also use things you meet every day at work as a source of useful language. Look at the letters received in your office, read any company literature which is written in English. Use the English around you to improve your English!

Don't just learn words; you also need to know how to use them. Which words does a word often combine with? This book will help you to learn more words, but also how to use the words you know more effectively. That is an important part of building your vocabulary.

Don't use your dictionary only when you have a problem. It is an important resource. It can help you in lots of different ways. There are tips all through this book to help you use your dictionary effectively.

Don't just make lists of new words; organise them. Again, there are tips to help you to learn and remember more of what you study.

Contents

1 Using a dictionary

If you want to learn business vocabulary, you should have a good English-English dictionary.
Use one with explanations that are easy to understand and which has sentences showing how you use the words.

Practise using a dictionary by answering these questions.

1. **Meaning**

   Which one of these would you get from a bank?

   depot   dial   dock   draft   drop

Of course a dictionary gives you a definition, but it helps you in other ways too. The next questions show you how.

2. **Words which go together**

Match a verb on the left with a noun on the right.

Use each word once only.

answer	a cheque	. . . .
attend	a computer	. . . .
cash	a conference	. . . .
join	the phone	. . . .
program	a team	. . . .

Some words often occur with other words; they form word partnerships. A good dictionary will give examples of the way in which words go together like this.

3. Word formation

Use the correct form of the word COMPETE in each sentence.

His . . . . are worried about his new range of products.

She took part in a . . . . to design a new yacht.

We have to be very . . . . to succeed in this business.

This car is more . . . . priced than the other one.

Words often have different grammatical forms. A good dictionary will show you these.

6

4. The past tense

Complete the sentence by using the past tense of the verb in brackets.

She . . . . $300 out of the bank. (DRAW)

In the past we . . . . the market in office equipment. (LEAD)

Last year profits . . . . by 20%. (RISE)

The strike soon . . . . to other departments. (SPREAD)

You need to know when a word is irregular; again your dictionary should help
you.

5. Abbreviations

What do the following abbreviations mean?

approx.   . . . .

Co.   . . . .

kg.   . . . .

FOB   . . . .

PO Box   . . . .

Abbreviations are used quite often in business so it is important to look up
and note down any new ones you meet. You should also know how to say
each abbreviation. A good dictionary should tell you this.

6. Pronunciation

Which of these words has a different vowel sound?

a.	gone	loan	own	phone
b.	fair	gear	share	wear
c.	could	food	goods	should
d.	freight	height	state	weight

You don't really know a word until you know how to say it properly. This is
why a good dictionary shows you the pronunciation of each word.

7

2 Word groups – 1

I t is useful to make a list of the words you use when you talk about a subject. When you learn a new word, you can add it to your list.
This book will give you some ideas but why not think of some areas of business you are interested in and see how many words you can think of?

Put each of the words below into the correct list.

Use each word once only.

Can you think of any more words to add to each list?

agenda	classified ad.	minutes	reservation
A.G.M.	commercial (n)	overtime	room service
apply for	exchange rate	owe	stapler
campaign	fax	poster	telex
chairperson	filing cabinet	profit	training
check in	interview	refund	weekend rate

1. **Advertising**

. . . .

. . . .

. . . .

. . . .

2. **Hotel**

. . . .

. . . .

. . . .

. . . .

3. **Job**

. . . .

. . . .

. . . .

. . . .

4. **Meeting**

. . . .

. . . .

. . . .

. . . .

5. **Money**

. . . .

. . . .

. . . .

. . . .

6. **The office**

. . . .

. . . .

. . . .

. . . .

3 In the office – 1

Look at the picture of an office. From the list below find the word for each numbered item. Use each word once only.

calendar	filing cabinet	pen	rubber (eraser)
cheque book	keyboard	pencil	umbrella
diary	map	phone	vase
files	passport	printer	VDU

1. . . . . 2. . . . . 3. . . . . 4. . . . .

5. . . . . 6. . . . . 7. . . . . 8. . . . .

9. . . . . 10. . . . . 11. . . . . 12. . . . .

13. . . . . 14. . . . . 15. . . . . 16. . . . .

4 Letters – 1 Enquiries

If you receive any business letters in English, use them to learn more vocabulary. Note down any useful words and phrases and then try to write similar letters of your own. In the same way, write your own letters based on those that you find in this book.

Below you will see parts of three letters of enquiry. Put the correct word or phrase in each blank. Choose from the following list. Use each item once only.

advertisement	discount	latest catalogue	price list
advise	faithfully	model	price range
current issue	forward	particularly	reference
Dear	information	payment	still available

A.

1. . . . . Sir

I have seen your 2. . . . . in the 3. . . . . of 'Office Weekly' and am interested in your range of office stationery.

Could you please send me your 4. . . . . and 5. . . . . I look 6. . . . . to hearing from you.

Yours 7. . . . .

B.

With 8. . . . . to your advertisement in today's 'Times', could you please send me 9. . . . . about your office furniture. I am 10. . . . . interested in your adjustable typist's chairs.

C.

Some time ago we purchased from you some JF72 solar-powered pocket calculators.

As this 11. . . . . was so popular with our customers, we would like to know if it is 12. . . . . If so, would you kindly 13. . . . . us of your terms of 14. . . . . and any quantity 15. . . . . available. Could you also include details of any new models in the same 16. . . . .

5 Word partnerships – 1

Some pairs of words often occur together. If you meet one, you can expect the other. This makes it easier to understand written and spoken English.

Match each verb on the left with a noun on the right to form common partnerships. Use each word once only. Write your answers in the boxes.

Set 1

1. answer	a. goods	**1**	
2. appoint	b. a letter	**2**	
3. arrange	c. a meeting	**3**	
4. export	d. a new manager	**4**	
5. pay	e. the phone	**5**	
6. solve	f. a problem	**6**	
7. type	g. tax	**7**	
8. welcome	h. a visitor	**8**	

Set 2

Now do the same with these words.

1. fill	a. an applicant	**1**	
2. interview	b. a business	**2**	
3. offer	c. a contract	**3**	
4. owe	d. a discount	**4**	
5. rent	e. some money	**5**	
6. run	f. office space	**6**	
7. send	g. a telex	**7**	
8. sign	h. a vacancy	**8**	

Now complete each sentence using a suitable expression from above.

1. They might . . . . if you pay within ten days.

2. Do you need a licence to . . . . to the Soviet Union?

3. Don't forget we have to . . . . on the profit we made.

4. I'm trying to . . . . with my bank manager next Tuesday.

6 Past tense – 1

M̲ost verbs in English form their past by adding 'd' or 'ed' but there are also about 200 irregular verbs in English. About 100 of these are common so you should always check the past tense of any verb you learn.

Complete each of the sentences by using the past form of one of the verbs on the left and combining it with one of the words on the right. Use each verb once only. Some words on the left are used more than once.

break	find	keep	shut		back	off	through
build	get	put	take		down	on	up
cut	go	read	think		forward	out	with
deal	hear	sell	ring		from	over	

1. By accident the switchboard operator . . . . her . . . . in the middle of our conversation.

2. After testing everything they finally . . . . what was wrong with the machine.

3. They . . . . costs . . . . by using less expensive materials.

4. The Finance Department . . . . the query about discounts.

5. He . . . . the figures . . . . to her so that she could be sure that he had the quantities exactly right.

6. She . . . . an interesting proposal at the meeting.

7. They . . . . the offer . . . . for a week before making a decision.

8. After ringing up three times I finally . . . . to head office.

9. She . . . . her business . . . . from one small shop to a chain of department stores.

10. The packing equipment . . . . and production was halted for an hour.

11. The new range was so popular that the shop . . . . in 2 days.

12. Last year they . . . . the factory for three weeks and everybody had to have their holiday at the same time.

13. She . . . . working even though the others had stopped.

14. I . . . . immediately saying I was interested in their offer.

15. My plane . . . . four hours late because of fog.

16. I finally . . . . our agent in Turkey. He phoned last week.

7 Using a trade directory

In a trade directory, services and suppliers are listed under appropriate headings.
In this exercise you have to decide which heading from the following list you would look under for what you need. Use each heading once only.
Write your answers in the boxes.

1. ACCOUNTANTS
2. ADVERTISING AGENCIES
3. AIR CHARTER & RENTAL
4. DEBT COLLECTORS
5. HOTELS
6. INTERIOR DESIGNERS

7. LAWYERS
8. OFFICE FURNITURE
9. RESTAURANT
10. SECURITY SERVICES
11. STATIONERY SUPPLIERS
12. TRAVEL AGENTS

PROBLEM

Problem	
a. You want to take a client out to dinner.	1
b. A visiting businessman wants somewhere to stay.	2
c. You're worried about your tax liabilities.	3
d. You're going to launch a new product onto the market.	4
e. You want to book a flight.	5
f. You're worried about industrial espionage.	6
g. You've run out of typing paper.	7
h. A typist needs a new chair.	8
i. Several customers have still not settled their accounts.	9
j. You want to hire a helicopter.	10
k. The reception area looks drab.	11
l. You are being sued for negligence.	12

Now complete each of the following sentences with a suitable phrase from the sentences you have just seen.

1. This new process is top secret and they're worried about . . . .

2. She's ringing the travel agency to . . . .

3. The clients who still hadn't . . . . were sent a final reminder.

4. They're holding a reception to . . . . onto the market.

5. Could you book a table at La Dolce Vita? I want to take Mr East . . . .

8 Confusing words – 1

If you use a word in the wrong way, learn from your mistake. Find out what the correct word or expression should be and then use both the correct and incorrect words in sentences so that you can understand and remember the differences.

Choose the correct word for each sentence.

1. She works for an **advertisement/advertising** agency.

2. How will the increase in interest rates **affect/effect** your sales?

3. My bank manager has agreed to **borrow/lend** me another $2,000.

4. We've had to **cancel/postpone** the meeting until next Monday.

5. These machines are **controlled/inspected** at least once a day.

6. My plane was **delayed/postponed** by an hour due to computer failure.

7. Before coming here, I studied **economics/economy** at university.

8. I am **interested/interesting** in their new camera.

9. She applied for a **job/work** as a personnel officer.

10. Some employees have a long **journey/travel** to work every day.

11. The cost of **life/living** has gone up again.

12. Please send precise **measurements/measures** when ordering.

13. We expect prices to **raise/rise** by at least five per cent.

14. We only exchange goods if you produce a **receipt/recipe**.

15. I must **remember/remind** the boss about that meeting this afternoon.

16. Can you **say/tell** the difference between these two products?

17. The company is extremely **sensible/sensitive** to any criticism.

18. There's some more paper in the **stationary/stationery** cupboard.

9 Banking services

One way of building your vocabulary is to ask yourself how many words you can write down about a certain subject. After you have made your list, and checked the spelling and pronunciation, you can add any new words you meet. Before you do this exercise, see how many words you can write down on the subject of banking. After you have done the exercise, add any new words to your list.

Fill each blank in the text with the correct word or phrase. Choose from the following list. Use each item once only.

commission	issued	statement	credit rating
debited	outstanding	withdraw	credit transfer
in full	salaries	banker's draft	financial institutions
interest	slip	cash dispenser	standing order

Banks offer many services to businesses and their customers. Here are some of the most common:

Many people now have a card which enables them to **1.**......... money from a **2.**......... You feed your card into the machine and key in your PIN (personal identification number) and the amount of money you want. If you have enough in your account, the money requested will be **3.**......... to you up to a daily limit. Your account is automatically **4.**......... for the amount you have drawn out.

Provided you have a sound **5.**........., you can get a credit card from a bank and other **6.**......... To obtain goods or services, you present your card and sign a special voucher. When it receives the voucher, the credit card company pays the trader (less a **7.**.........) and then sends you a monthly **8.**......... Depending on the type of card you have, you will either have to pay **9.**......... or be able to pay part of what is owed and pay **10.**......... on the balance left **11.**.........

If you need to make fixed payments at regular intervals, e.g. for insurance premiums, you can arrange a **12.**......... (sometimes known as a banker's order) so that the bank will do this for you.

If you have several bills to pay, you can do this by **13.**......... You write one cheque for the total sum involved, fill in a **14.**......... for each bill and hand everything to the bank cashier.

The transfer system is also used by employers to pay **15.**......... directly into employees' bank accounts.

If you are dealing with a supplier for the first time, a **16.**......... may be used as payment. This is a cheque guaranteed by a bank and therefore it is not likely to 'bounce'.

10 Social English – 1

In business there are times when you need to speak English socially, for
example when you go out for a meal with an English-speaking client or
colleague. It is important, therefore, to know some of the expressions used in
these more informal situations. As you do this exercise, try to imagine
situations in which these exchanges could occur.

Complete each of these conversations with an appropriate response from the list
below. Use each response once only.

Responses

a. Pleased to meet you. I'm Jane Ford.
b. Oh, so soon?
c. Thanks. You too.
d. Congratulations!
e. Not at all. It's been a pleasure.
f. No thanks. I've just had one.
g. Yes, very much, thanks.
h. No better, I'm afraid.
i. Only a few days.
j. Yes it is, isn't it.
k. That would be very nice, thanks.
l. Is there anything I can do to help?

1. . . . .

2. . . . .

3. . . . .

4. . . . .

5. . . . .

6. . . . .

7. . . . .

8. . . . .

9. . . . .

10. . . . .

11. . . . .

12. . . . .

17

11 Letters – 2
Answering enquiries

Below you will see parts of three letters answering an enquiry. Put the correct word or phrase in each blank. Choose from the following list. Use each item once only.

additional features	enclosed leaflet	further details	pleasure
competitive price	enquiring	hesitate	range
date	enquiry	In addition	sincerely
doing business	full details	in production	supply

A.

Dear Ms Prentice

Thank you for your **1.** . . . . of 3rd May about our office stationery.

We have **2.** . . . . in enclosing our latest catalogue and price list. We hope you will find it of interest.

If you require any **3.** . . . . , please do not **4.** . . . . to contact us.

Yours **5.** . . . .

B.

Thank you for your letter of January 4th, asking about office furniture.

The enclosed catalogue contains **6.** . . . . of our range. In most cases we are able to **7.** . . . . you with the goods you require within fourteen days.

We look forward to receiving an order from you.

C.

Thank you for your letter of 1st June, **8.** . . . . about the JF72 pocket calculator.

This model is no longer **9.** . . . . as it has been superseded by the JF73 solar-powered pocket calculator. As you will see from the **10.** . . . . , the new model has several **11.** . . . . at an extremely **12.** . . . .

We have also enclosed our latest catalogue giving details of the vast **13.** . . . . of electronic goods we supply.

We allow a discount of 30% on purchases of not less than 50 of the same model, and 35% on quantities of not less than 100. **14.** . . . . , we give a discount of 3% for payment within fourteen days from **15.** . . . . of invoice.

We look forward to **16.** . . . . with you in the near future.

12 Two-word expressions – 1

Sometimes in English two words are used together to make a common expression, for example:

credit card   **departure lounge**

Sometimes you will find these expressions listed separately in a dictionary and sometimes they are included in the definitions of one, or both, of the words. You need to learn the expressions as complete phrases.

Join one word on the left with one from the right to make a two-word partnership. Use each word once only. Write your answers in the boxes.

1. box	a. block		1	
2. cash	b. board		2	
3. civil	c. cabinet		3	
4. economy	d. drive		4	
5. exchange	e. exchange		5	
6. filing	f. flow		6	
7. income	g. margin		7	
8. insurance	h. number		8	
9. job	i. policy		9	
10. notice	j. processor		10	
11. office	k. rate		11	
12. profit	l. satisfaction		12	
13. stock	m. service		13	
14. trade	n. tax		14	
15. word	o. union		15	

Now complete each sentence with one of the expressions.

1. She bought a . . . . to replace her old typewriter.

2. They built a big . . . . in the middle of town.

3. Change your money when the . . . . is more favourable.

4. For some people . . . . is more important than a high salary.

19

13 Product information

If you can get catalogues in English, or magazines or newspapers containing advertisements in English, look at the descriptions of the products. You can find a lot of useful vocabulary in this way.

In addition, many products have information written in English which will also help you to build your vocabulary. Remember, there are many opportunities to see real English. All of them can help you to learn.

In this exercise you will see some information about a product. You must decide which product is being referred to. Choose the product from the following list. Each product is referred to once only.

answer phone	computer	laser printer	photocopier
briefcase	cordless phone	office chair	pocket calculator
burglar alarm	diary	partitioning	signmaking kit
clock	fax machine	pen	table lamp

Desk top publishing at an economical price. High resolution. Compatible with a wide range of systems.	With built-in pre-recorded message or facility to record your own. Speaker volume control.

1. . . . . 2. . . . .

The infa-red sensors detect any intruders. A message is immediately sent to the control	Make calls anywhere inside or within 100 metres outside. Paging facility.

3. . . . . 4. . . . .

60 grey shades for better transmission of photographs. One touch dialling.	High resolution colour monitor. Comes complete with word-processing and other business software.

5. . . . . 6. . . . .

Stylish cover. Page a day. Contains conversion tables and other useful information.	Swivel base. With or without arms. Fully adjustable. Variety of fabrics. Extra deep cushioning.

7. . . . .   **8.** . . . .

Large quantity in stock. Immediate delivery. Dismantling and erecting service available.	The effective answer to high volume duplication. Adjustable speeds. Quality reproduction.

9. . . . .   **10.** . . . .

Durable self-adhesive letters, numbers and symbols in a variety of sizes. Can be used indoors and out.	White dial with black numerals. Battery supplied.

11. . . . .   **12.** . . . .

Document folio in lid. Pockets for calculator, pens etc. Combination locks.	Solar powered. 8-digit LCD display.

13. . . . .   **14.** . . . .

Stainless steel cap and barrel. Supplied with blue refill.	Fully adjustable. Reach 30 in. Max 60 watt bulb.

15. . . . .   **16.** . . . .

Now look through the descriptions and note down any words or phrases that will be useful for you.

14 Word formation – 1

When you look up a word in a dictionary, see if you can form other words from it. Sometimes these words will be included in the definition of the word and sometimes they will appear separately. Look before and after each dictionary entry to see what words you can find formed from the same basic word.

Complete each sentence with the correct form of the word in capital letters. In some cases you will have to make a negative form by using the prefix **in-** or **un-**.

1. ACCEPT

    I'm sorry, but this arrangement is totally . . . . to us.

    I've just received their letter of . . . . so we can go ahead.

2. ACT

    The unions have threatened to take industrial . . . .

    It's been a very . . . . day on the Stock Exchange.

    The R&D department seems full of . . . . at the moment.

3. ADD

    We'll be bringing out several . . . . to our product line.

    There's an . . . . bonus if I exceed my sales target by more than 10%.

4. ANALYSE

    We'll need a detailed cost . . . . before giving final approval.

    Most . . . . think we're in for a difficult time.

5. APPLY

    Unfortunately we can't interview every . . . .

    I sent in my letter of . . . . and they phoned me the next day.

    The regulations are not . . . . when there are fewer than 10 employees.

6. ASSIST

    We'll need some financial . . . . to enable us to buy more stock.

    He was in a meeting so I spoke to the . . . . manager.

7. ATTRACT

    One of the . . . . of the offer is the free training course.

    They were offering a very . . . . salary so of course I was interested.

8. COMMERCE

There are so many . . . . vehicles on the road these days!

I'm afraid the scheme is not . . . . viable.

The resort has become so . . . . that we're going somewhere else.

As well as newspaper advertising, we plan a series of TV . . . .

9. CONNECT

My . . . . flight didn't leave until 10 o'clock.

We sent them a letter in . . . . with their offer of an agency.

She has some useful . . . . in the hotel trade.

10. CONTRACT

The . . . . has told me the office will be ready by next month.

We are . . . . obliged to provide adequate security for the shipment.

11. DIRECT

I enclose a map and . . . . to help you to find our office.

The board of . . . . will make the final decision about the scheme.

I found the company by looking in the local trade . . . .

I always deal . . . . with the manufacturer.

There's been another . . . . from head office about photocopying.

12. DECIDE

He'll never make a good manager. He's so . . . .

A . . . . on the new factory is expected soon.

13. DIFFER

Installing air-conditioning has made all the . . . .

We've decided to try a . . . . supplier this time.

We'll have to agree to . . . . I still think it would be better to go by road.

14. DISTRIBUTE

He's the sole . . . . in this area, so we're forced to buy from him.

The increase in petrol prices will push up our . . . . costs.

15. ECONOMY

We must . . . . on electricity, so switch off those lights.

All those wonderful . . . . haven't found a solution to our problems.

23

15 Opposites – 1

When you see an adjective in a sentence, ask yourself if it is possible to replace it by its opposite. You will notice that some adjectives have several opposites depending on the context.

The opposite of *short*, for example, could be *long* or *tall*. Can you think of any more examples like this? A good dictionary will help you. It's another word partnership problem!

Complete each sentence with the opposite of the word in brackets. Choose from the following list. Use each word once only.

approximate	full-time	marked	private
basic	internal	negative	short
complex	light	partial	
compulsory	low	permanent	

1. The new complaints procedure has been a . . . . success. (COMPLETE)

2. Have you got the . . . . sales figures? (EXACT)

3. The post went to an . . . . candidate. (EXTERNAL)

4. I didn't expect my salary to be as . . . . as this! (HIGH)

5. There's a lot of . . . . industry in the area. (HEAVY)

6. We're expecting big savings in the . . . . term. (LONG)

7. Wearing a tie was . . . . in his office. (OPTIONAL)

8. She has a . . . . job as a shorthand typist. (PART-TIME)

9. There was a very . . . . reaction to my suggestion. (POSITIVE)

10. Wages have risen more slowly in the . . . . sector. (PUBLIC)

11. The company has a . . . . management structure. (SIMPLE)

12. There was a . . . . improvement in efficiency. (SLIGHT)

13. We could see he was using very . . . . equipment. (SOPHISTICATED)

14. He's got himself a . . . . job as a mechanic. (TEMPORARY)

16 Word partnerships – 2

Match each adjective on the left with a noun on the right to form common partnerships. Use each word once only. Write your answers in the boxes.

Set 1

1. annual	a. conference		1	
2. early	b. credit		2	
3. extended	c. dismissal		3	
4. limited	d. enterprise		4	
5. natural	e. liability		5	
6. occupational	f. pension		6	
7. private	g. resources		7	
8. unfair	h. retirement		8	

Set 2

Now do the same with these words.

1. effective	a. communication		1	
2. financial	b. difficulties		2	
3. high	c. investment		3	
4. introductory	d. offer		4	
5. skilled	e. priority		5	
6. sound	f. property		6	
7. vacant	g. range		7	
8. wide	h. workers		8	

Now complete each sentence using an appropriate expression from above.

1. As a special . . . . , they're selling two for the price of one.

2. I'm going to the . . . . of our trade union.

3. He was only 50 but he decided to take . . . .

4. There is a shortage of . . . . for this kind of work.

25

17 Mr Baker's trip

Below you will see pictures of different stages in Mr Baker's trip. You must decide which of the sentences below goes with which picture. Use each sentence once only.

a. Thanks very much for all your help.

b. I've got an appointment with Miss Jarvis.

c. I'd like to book a room with a bath in the name of Baker.

d. Keep the change.

e. This is the last call for flight QF2, now boarding at Gate 24.

f. How was your trip?

g. Have you got anything to declare, sir?

h. A return to Ashfield, please.

i. Medium, please.

j. The Hotel Major, please.

k. My name's Baker. My secretary has booked a room for me.

l. Pleased to meet you.

m. Here's to our continued co-operation.

n. I'm afraid there's been a mistake. I'm sure my secretary booked a room with bath.

1. . . . .

2. . . . .

3. . . . .

4. . . . .

5. . . . .
6. . . . .

7. . . . .
8. . . . .

9. . . . .
10. . . . .

11. . . . .
12. . . . .

13. . . . .
14. . . . .

18 Letters – 3 Orders

Below you will see parts of four letters concerned with orders. Put the correct word or phrase in each blank. Choose from the following list. Use each item once only.

accept delivery	inconvenience	range	quotation
acknowledge	line	regret	stock
current issue	note	reserve the right	supply
following	postage	resume	terms

A.

With reference to your advertisement in the **1.**........of 'Office Monthly', I would like to order 2 Easifix Year Planners.
I enclose a cheque for £15 to include **2.**........and packing.

B.

Thank you for your **3.**........of 5th July for your "Finesse" **4.**........of dining room furniture. We find your **5.**........satisfactory and would like to order the **6.**........ .

    10 "Finesse" dining tables at £280 per item
    40 "Finesse" dining chairs at £60 per item

We **7.**........that you can supply these items within 30 days and we **8.**........not to **9.**........after this time.
We should be obliged if you would **10.**........receipt of this order.

C.

We thank you for your order of 11th May for 2 Easifix Year Planners.
This **11.**........has proved so popular that we **12.**........to inform you that it is temporarily out of stock.
We hope to be able to **13.**........supplies within the next ten days.
We apologise for any **14.**........this may cause.

D.

Thank you for your order of 12th July for 10 "Finesse" dining tables and 40 "Finesse" dining chairs.
As we are in a position to **15.**........you with the above items from **16.**........, we have arranged for them to be delivered to you early next week.

19 Word groups – 2

R emember that grouping together words connected with the same topic can help you to learn them. As you meet new vocabulary, see if you can think of other words that could be used in the same context.

Put each of the words below into the correct list.
Some words could go into more than one list but use each word once only and put it into the category with which it is most commonly associated.
Can you think of any more words to add to each list?

actuary	dumping	picket	speculate
bears	embargo	policyholder	stock exchange
claim	export	premium	strike
closed shop	judge	program	sue
compatible	legal	shares	tariff
data	mediate	software	trial

1. Computers

. . . .

. . . .

. . . .

. . . .

2. Industrial relations

. . . .

. . . .

. . . .

. . . .

3. Insurance

. . . .

. . . .

. . . .

. . . .

4. International trade

. . . .

. . . .

. . . .

. . . .

5. Investing

. . . .

. . . .

. . . .

. . . .

6. The law

. . . .

. . . .

. . . .

. . . .

20 The electronic office

In this passage about the use of computers in business you must fill each blank with one word. Choose each word from the following list. You must use each word once only.

accurate	input	printer	screen
components	keyboard	modem	single
continuous	linked	records	supplies
floppy	output	retrieve	transactions

USING COMPUTERS

Computers are being used more and more in business because they are fast, efficient and **1.** . . . .

Here are some ways in which computers are used:

Insurance companies use them to store and **2.** . . . . details of clients' policies.

Production departments in companies use them to ensure they have adequate **3.** . . . . of raw materials and **4.** . . . .

Banks use them for processing details of accounts and **5.** . . . .

Personnel departments use them to keep **6.** . . . . of a company's employees.

Can you think of any other ways in which computers are used?

The most common ways in which you can **7.** . . . . information into a computer are:

- by typing it on a **8.** . . . .
- from a **9.** . . . . disk
- by **10.** . . . . over a telephone link.
- from another computer **11.** . . . . to yours.

A computer can **12.** . . . . information:

- on a **13.** . . . . called a VDU (visual display unit).
- to a **14.** . . . . which may use **15.** . . . . sheets or
  16. . . . . stationery.
- to a floppy disk.
- to another computer.

21 Make or do?

Complete each sentence with the correct form of 'make' or 'do'.

1. There's a rumour going round that Pelly's are going to . . . . a bid for Squash International.

2. Please . . . . your best to get these typed before 5 o'clock.

3. Who shall I . . . . the cheque out to?

4. If we don't get some orders soon we'll have to . . . . some of our workers redundant.

5. I'm afraid you'll have to . . . . without the other photocopier until we can get the part we need from the suppliers.

6. We've been . . . . business with them for over thirty years now.

7. Considerable progress has been . . . . and we hope to put some concrete proposals to our members tomorrow afternoon.

8. The bank has decided to . . . . extra provision against bad debts this year.

9. They've been . . . . a roaring trade since they decided to advertise on local television.

10. We have . . . . a considerable profit on the sale of that land.

11. I've got all these invoices to . . . . before I can go home.

12. The business was so run down when she took it over that nobody expected her to . . . . such a success of it.

13. Something as simple as changing the size of the lettering on the packet can . . . . all the difference to your sales.

14. Increasing production will . . . . even more demands on machinery which is already breaking down at an alarming rate.

15. They could . . . . with some computer paper in the wages office.

16. We've . . . . away with the old system of clocking in.

17. A customer has . . . . a complaint about one of our salespeople.

18. In fact, Gravers have . . . . us a favour by launching their product first. We can learn from their mistakes.

When you have checked your answers, underline each expression with 'do' or 'make' to help you to remember them.

22 Problems, problems

My typist keeps complaining
of backache.
– If I were you, I'd get
her a better chair.

Match each sentence below with the best response on the next page.
Use each response once only.

1. . . . .

2. . . . .

3. . . . .

4. . . . .

5. . . . .

6. . . . .

7. . . . .

8. . . . .

9. . . . .

10. . . . .

11. . . . .

12. . . . .

a. Let's see what R & D can come up with.
b. Shall I get you some more from the stationery store?
c. Why don't you look for a job abroad?
d. Have you tried getting one from an employment agency?
e. They say there's still growth left in the leisure industry.
f. How about Tuesday morning?

g. I'd give them another ring if I were you.
h. Do you think arbitration would help?
i. Maybe they'll accept part payment.
j. In that case, you'd better send it registered.
k. Do you want me to look through them for you?
l. Why not fax them, then?

33

23 Letters – 4 Delayed orders

Below you will see parts of three letters concerned with a delay in fulfilling an order. Put the correct word or phrase in each blank. Choose from the following list. Use each item once only.

apologise for	deter	mislaid	refund
dealing	further delay	obliged	regret the delay
deducted	issue	passed	reply
despatching	matter	promised delivery	set

A.

On 8th October I sent you an order for a 1......... of five computer programs which you had advertised in the October 2......... of 'Computer World'.

Although your advertisement 3......... within 28 days, 6 weeks have now 4......... and I have still not received the programs. You must have received my order as the £70 I paid by cheque has been 5......... from my bank account.

Would you please look into this 6......... for me and send my order without 7......... .

B.

Two weeks ago I sent you a letter inquiring about my order of 8th October for five computer programs which had not arrived.

I have received no 8......... to my letter and the programs have still not been delivered. I must ask you, therefore, either to send my order immediately or to 9......... my payment of £70.

I hope I shall not be 10......... to take this matter any further.

C.

Thank you for your letter of November 23rd. We 11......... in 12......... your order for the five computer programs.

Unfortunately, we had problems with our new computerised system for 13......... with orders and, as a result, your order was 14......... .

We have enclosed the five programs you ordered together with an extra disk which we hope will go some way to making up for the delay.

Once again we 15......... the inconvenience. We hope that it will not 16......... you from doing business with us in the future.

24 Special areas – 1
Buying and selling

Choose the best alternative to complete the sentence.

1. As soon as an item of stock falls below its minimum . . . . , the computer automatically re-orders.
   a. standard   **b.** level   **c.** grade   **d.** position

2. Often a discount is offered as an . . . . to get a customer to pay promptly.
   a. investment   **b.** incentive   **c.** interim   **d.** inventory

3. Remember that was only an . . . . The final cost could be higher.
   a. enquiry   **b.** estimate   **c.** encouragement **d.** engagement

4. Check the . . . . note and see that you've got everything.
   a. deliver   **b.** delivered   **c.** delivery   **d.** delivering

5. When ordering, please quote the . . . .
   a. numbered catalogue   **b.** catalogue   **c.** figure   **d.** catalogue number

6. I've just received an . . . . note telling me that the goods have been dispatched.
   a. advice   **b.** advise   **c.** invoice   **d.** advisory

7. Every month account customers are sent a . . . .
   a. final demand   **b.** statement **c.** request   **d.** stocktaking

8. In the UK, VAT (value added tax) is a tax on goods and . . . .
   a. services   **b.** servants   **c.** stockings   **d.** stockists

9. If they don't . . . . their account we'll take them to court.
   a. set up   **b.** pay up   **c.** settle   **d.** pay for

10. By mistake we have undercharged her so we'll have to send her a . . . . note for the amount.
    a. debt   **b.** credit   **c.** debit   **d.** credit-worthy

11. If you take the sweater back to the shop they'll want to see the . . . . to show you bought it there.
    a. receipt   **b.** reception   **c.** permit   **d.** quotation

12. It's a . . . . market at the moment so you should be able to pick some up at a reasonable price.
    a. open   **b.** free   **c.** buyer's   **d.** seller's

13. The market has reached . . . . point so we need to concentrate on finding new products.
    a. full   **b.** saturation **c.** filling   **d.** boiling

14. We hope that business will . . . . when the tourist season starts.
    a. set off   **b.** get up   **c.** pick up   **d.** pick off

15. You'll probably find furniture polish among the . . . . goods.
    a. house   **b.** housing   **c.** household   **d.** housewife

16. They've pulled down the old market and built a shopping . . . .
    a. premises   **b.** precinct   **c.** franchise   **d.** retailer

25 The passive

As you read about business in newspapers and magazines, notice how often the passive form is used in sentences such as:

Grove Developments **have been chosen** to build the new sports centre.

It is important that you know the past participle form of every verb you learn as this will help you to understand and make sentences in which the passive is used.

In this exercise you have to complete each sentence by using the correct form of one of the following verbs. Use each verb once only.

build	make	send	take over
hold	overcome	set up	tell
know	say	spend	underwrite
lose	sell	steal	win

1. More than 6 million tins of beans are . . . . every week.

2. They were . . . . by an American company last year.

3. No attempt was . . . . to explain the inconsistency in the figures.

4. Kent Industries are . . . . to be thinking of expanding overseas.

5. Once initial problems had been . . . . the re-organisation went like clockwork.

6. Their new factory will be . . . . on the outskirts of town.

7. The contract was . . . . in the face of strong competition.

8. Over $3 million was . . . . on advertising last year.

9. A prospectus will be . . . . to all potential investors.

10. Why weren't clients . . . . in advance about this increase in fees?

11. A product can be . . . . by different names in different countries.

12. An extraordinary general meeting will be . . . . next Wednesday.

13. The share offer will be . . . . by a leading merchant bank.

14. 110 working days have been . . . . so far this year as a result of industrial unrest.

15. A network of service centres will be . . . . to take care of installation and maintenance.

16. They claim that plans for the new aircraft were . . . . by a competitor.

26 Organisation chart

T hink about the ways in which companies are organised into departments with different responsibilities. Do you know the names in English of the people in charge and how to talk about their responsibilities? If not, try to find out and then make your own chart similar to the one below.

Below you will see a chart showing the way in which a company could be organised. In some cases, a word is missing from the chart. Find the correct word from the following list. Use each word once only. Write your answers at the bottom of the page.

Accountant	Control	Manager	Processing
Administration	Head	Managing	Recruitment
Advertising	Innovation	Market	Salaries
Board	Mail	Personnel	Stock

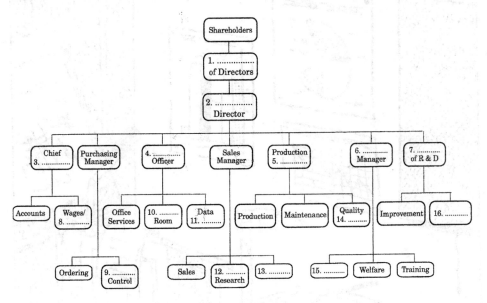

The missing words are:

1. . . . .   2. . . . .   3. . . . .   4. . . . .

5. . . . .   6. . . . .   7. . . . .   8. . . . .

9. . . . .   10. . . . .   11. . . . .   12. . . . .

13. . . . .   14. . . . .   15. . . . .   16. . . . .

37

27 Making a presentation

A.

Look at the picture. Put the correct number by each of these items.

bar chart	felt pen	handout . . . .
pointer	curtain	flip chart . . . .
pie chart	screen	slide projector . . . .
notes	podium	overhead projector . . . .
graph	microphone	

38

B.

Below you will see extracts from a presentation. You must complete each blank with a word or phrase from the list below. Use each item from the list once only.

purpose	First of all,	up to date	at such short notice
priorities	May I begin	to sum up	On the contrary,
Finally,	As you know,	as a whole	On the other hand,
Next,	In other words,	As far as	draw your attention

1......... by welcoming you all, especially as this meeting has had to be called
2.......... .

3........., our latest project has been the target of intense speculation in the media during the last few days, and the 4........ of this presentation is to bring you 5........ on what has been happening.

6........, I'd like to refresh your memories as to the background to the project. 7........, I'll give you a broad outline of what we've achieved so far.
8........, I'll try to give an indication of what our 9........ will be over the next few months.

If I can 10........ to the month of July, you will notice that there was an unexpected fall in overseas sales.

11........ domestic sales are concerned, you can see that growth has been sustained.

If we look at the figures for Europe 12........, and Germany in particular, we can see some quite encouraging trends.

We don't fear competition. 13........, we welcome it.

We could open a branch there. 14........, we may be better advised to look for a good agent to represent us.

This is a time when we must consider our options carefully. 15........, we should not rush into making any decisions.

So, 16........ then, don't believe everything the media tells you. We've had a few problems but the future looks bright.

28 Word partnerships – 3

Match each verb on the left with a noun on the right to form common partnerships. Use each word once only. Write your answers in the boxes.

Set 1

1. address	**a.** a client	**1**	
2. arrange	**b.** a demonstration	**2**	
3. consider	**c.** an employee	**3**	
4. fire	**d.** an invoice	**4**	
5. keep	**e.** a meeting	**5**	
6. pay	**f.** an order	**6**	
7. place	**g.** a proposal	**7**	
8. phone	**h.** a record	**8**	

Set 2

Now do the same with these words.

1. build	**a.** agreement	**1**	
2. cash	**b.** a cheque	**2**	
3. despatch	**c.** costs	**3**	
4. express	**d.** disputes	**4**	
5. postpone	**e.** a factory	**5**	
6. reach	**f.** goods	**6**	
7. reduce	**g.** a meeting	**7**	
8. settle	**h.** thanks	**8**	

Now complete each sentence by using a suitable expression from above.

1. They hope to . . . . by employing fewer staff.

2. Could you . . . . so we can see exactly how it works?

3. It's not always easy to . . . . between management and staff.

4. They're going to . . . . on some vacant land nearby.

40

29 Choose the adverb – 1

As you study English, notice how some adverbs form common partnerships with other words, for example:

Each product is **thoroughly tested.**   This process is **widely used.**

If you want to use English in a natural way, you should note down and learn expressions like this.

From the following list choose a suitable adverb to complete each sentence. Use each adverb once only.

absolutely	correctly	fully	tactfully
actively	eventually	satisfactorily	temporarily
considerably	favourably	specially	virtually
conveniently	financially	strictly	widely

1. Our new office is . . . . located in the middle of town.

2. I hope the negotiations will be concluded . . . .

3. This credit card is . . . . accepted so I take it everywhere.

4. Make sure you're . . . . insured when you go to the States.

5. The accountant had to check that the company was . . . . sound.

6. You have been . . . . selected to try out our latest product.

7. I'm sure the Government's policy will . . . . cause a recession.

8. Get this software . . . . free when you buy one of our computers.

9. Entry to this part of the factory is . . . . limited.

10. Production methods vary . . . . from firm to firm.

11. Make sure the envelope is . . . . addressed.

12. The switchboard is . . . . out of order but it'll be soon fixed.

13. The tableware they produce is . . . . unbreakable.

14. She learned how to deal . . . . with people who complained.

15. Our sales figures compare . . . . with those of our competitors.

16. Staff should be . . . . encouraged to show initiative.

30 Special areas – 2
Public relations

Choose the best alternative to complete the sentence.

1. The task of the public relations department is to project the right . . . .
   of a company.
   a. painting **b.** image **c.** picture **d.** drawing

2. When the product was launched they issued a press . . . . to all the
   news agencies.
   a. escape **b.** issue **c.** release **d.** promotion

3. According to the code of practice, a public relations officer should not
   knowingly . . . . false information.
   a. disseminate **b.** dissociate **c.** dispose **d.** dissolve

4. Some companies entertain journalists more . . . . than others.
   a. lasciviously **b.** largely **c.** leniently **d.** lavishly

5. The use of such things as logos and colour . . . . helps to maintain a
   corporate identity.
   a. schemes **b.** systems **c.** styles **d.** fashions

6. We need to liaise more with politicians and . . . . , servants if we want
   the government to agree to our plans.
   a. official **b.** polite **c.** civil **d.** civilian

7. $200,000 was . . . . for the official opening of the new store.
   a. set aside **b.** brought about **c.** set off **d.** laid up

8. Sponsorship can be an effective way of promoting . . . . towards an
   organisation.
   a. will **b.** goodwill **c.** willingness **d.** goodness

9. At a press reception don't . . . . guests with irrelevant material.
   a. overload **b.** override **c.** overtake **d.** overcompensate

10. The reception must be held at a convenient . . . . with good transport
    and parking facilities.
    a. revue **b.** venue **c.** view **d.** venture

11. When making a presentation to a relatively small . . . . an overhead
    projector can be invaluable.
    a. assistance **b.** spectator **c.** audience **d.** congregation

12. Within a large organisation a well-designed . . . . journal is an effective
    method of internal communication.
    a. in-house **b.** home **c.** household **d.** plant

13. Participating in local events, such as carnivals, is a good way of developing
    . . . . relations.
    a. common **b.** commonplace **c.** communal **d.** community

14. We used every . . . . of communication to get our message across.
    a. flow **b.** stream **c.** channel **d.** canal

15. We have to highlight our strengths and . . . . any weaknesses.
    a. play up **b.** think through **c.** play down **d.** talk back

31 Letters – 5 Sales

Below you will see extracts from three sales letters. Put the correct word or phrase in each blank. Choose from the following list. Use each item once only.

colleagues	featured	complimentary copy	recent publications
confident	needs	extensively trialled	representatives
convenience	recommend	favourable response	specially selected
eligible	suitable	further information	subscription form
experience	value	highly popular	terms of payment

A.

We have pleasure in enclosing a 1.........of one of our most 2........., 'Build Your Business Vocabulary'.

You will note that the book has a similar format to our 3........series, 'Build Your Vocabulary', but concentrates on vocabulary useful to anyone who needs English in a business situation.

The exercises have been 4........and have met with a 5........from both learners and teachers. The book is 6........for use in the classroom or by a learner of English working alone.

We feel sure that you will want to 7........this book to your colleagues and students.

B.

We are a company with over 30 years 8........in selling office equipment. We have recently brought out a new range of equipment and furniture designed to meet the 9........of today's electronic office.

This new range is 10........in our latest brochure which I have enclosed together with details of our generous 11......... .

If you require any 12........., simply telephone me and I will arrange for one of our 13........to call on you.

C.

You have been 14........ by my company to receive a free copy of our latest publication 'Business Dealings'.

We cannot of course send a free copy to everyone but we have chosen you because we 15........ your opinion. We are 16........ that you will find it fascinating and want to show it to your 17......... .

'Business Dealings' is published monthly and we have enclosed a 18........ for your 19........ Subscribe within the next three weeks and you will be 20........ for a discount of twenty per cent.

32 Advertising – 1

In advertising, the right choice of words can help to sell a product. If possible, look at some advertisements in English and see how many word partnerships you can find which create a favourable impression of the product.

Match each word on the left with a word on the right. Use each word once only. Write your answers in the boxes.

Set 1

1. competitive	a. brochure	**1**	
2. delicious	b. cleaning	**2**	
3. effortless	c. details	**3**	
4. finest	d. fit	**4**	
5. full	e. flavours	**5**	
6. glossy	f. quality	**6**	
7. perfect	g. rates	**7**	
8. wide	h. variety	**8**	

Set 2

Now do the same with these words.

1. forward-looking	a. brochure	**1**	
2. full-colour	b. company	**2**	
3. hard-wearing	c. driving	**3**	
4. highly-trained	d. recipes	**4**	
5. money-saving	e. shoes	**5**	
6. mouth-watering	f. spray	**6**	
7. ozone-friendly	g. staff	**7**	
8. stress-free	h. tips	**8**	

Now complete each sentence by using an expression from above.

1. Inside each cooker there's a free cook book full of . . . .

2. Our . . . . are ready to look after your every need.

3. With hand-made shoes you get a . . . . every time.

4. The sophisticated automatic steering means . . . .

33 Opposites – 2

Y ou can often build your vocabulary by asking yourself if you know the opposite of one of the most important words in a sentence.

It also helps to learn words in a complete sentence. This makes them easier to remember.

Complete each sentence with the opposite of the word in brackets.
Choose from the following list. Use each word once only.
You must use the correct form of the verb.

accept	demolish	increase	reject
agree	expand	keep	strengthen
attack	gain	lose	succeed
complicate	impose	lower	withdraw

1. He's . . . . my recommendation. (ACCEPTED)

2. They're . . . . an office block down by the river. (CONSTRUCTING)

3. She . . . . the company's policy on the environment. (DEFENDED)

4. She's gone to the bank to . . . . some money. (DEPOSIT)

5. Is he the kind of person to . . . . his responsibilities? (EVADE)

6. I think his reorganisation plan will ultimately . . . . (FAIL)

7. They've . . . . restrictions on using the telex. (LIFTED)

8. Share prices . . . . ground throughout the day. (LOST)

9. We . . . . a lot of money on that last deal. (MADE)

10. Did he . . . . his appointment with that journalist? (MISS)

11. They say the banks are going to . . . . interest rates. (RAISE)

12. I think this move will . . . . the deficit. (REDUCE)

13. Won't the new clocking-in system . . . . things? (SIMPLIFY)

14. Getting outside finance can only . . . . our position. (WEAKEN)

15. Ship-building has . . . . in this area over the years. (DECLINED)

16. He . . . . that the company was in trouble. (DENIED)

45

34 Word formation – 2

Complete each sentence with the correct form of the word in capital letters. In some cases you will have to make a negative by using the prefix **il-**, **mis-** or **un-**.

1. EMPLOY

In an area of high . . . . people are desperate to find jobs.

Every . . . . of the firm is entitled to a 10% discount.

Her . . . . gets very angry if she uses the phone too much.

I'm looking for temporary . . . . during the summer holidays.

2. ENGAGE

The line is . . . . so I'll have to try again later.

Cancel all my . . . . for the rest of the day, please.

3. EXPENSE

It's . . . . to send the goods by air but they're needed urgently.

They offered her £15,000 plus . . . .

Unfortunately, ... on the project was much more than expected.

His . . . . claims are being looked at by the Chief Accountant.

4. EXPLAIN

If you read the . . . . leaflet, everything should become clear.

We're waiting for an . . . . of his behaviour in the meeting.

5. EXTEND

We've decided to agree to their request for . . . . credit.

Could I speak to Miss Charles, please? I think it's . . . . 272.

The factory was . . . . damaged in the fire.

To some . . . . I agree with her conclusions.

6. FINANCE

Her . . . . adviser is convinced the project will be a success.

If the company is . . . . sound we might consider taking it over.

7. GROW

There is a . . . . awareness of the need to improve productivity.

The government is worried about the . . . . in public expenditure.

46

8. IMPRESS

It's important to create a good . . . . when meeting clients.

The results from our new French subsidiary are very . . . .

I'm afraid she was . . . . by our presentation.

9. INDUSTRY

In this high-tech world, ... espionage is on the increase.

Mr Fredericks, a prominent . . . ., will head the committee of inquiry.

In some of the more . . . . countries pollution is a big problem.

10. INFLATE

I've no intention of paying such . . . . prices!

At the moment . . . . is running at 20%.

The government must take steps to halt the . . . . spiral.

11. INFORM

Please let me know if you need any more . . . .

I enjoyed her talk. It was very . . . .

I'm afraid you've been . . . . She no longer works for us.

12. INSTRUCT

The boss has left . . . . that she's not to be disturbed.

I can't make head nor tail of this . . . . manual!

13. INTRODUCE

The chairman made some . . . . remarks and then she gave her talk.

I'd like to welcome Jane Phipps, who, I'm sure, needs no . . . .

14. INVEST

These shares have given me a good return on my . . . .

Small . . . . were advised to hold on to their shares.

15. KNOW

We need somebody with a good working . . . . of French.

Our company is virtually . . . . abroad.

She's obviously very . . . . as far as marketing is concerned.

16. LEGAL

It's . . . . to sell such goods without a proper permit.

They questioned the . . . . of the company's action.

35 Formal English

I n some business letters and legal documents – more formal English is used. For example, although somebody might say:

We're trying to find out where she is.

in formal English this might be written as:

We are endeavouring to ascertain her whereabouts.

This is a rather extreme example as there has been a reaction against this type of language. However, it is still important to recognise this kind of formal language and to know its less formal equivalent.

Complete each sentence by using each word from the following list. At the end of each sentence write its less formal equivalent. Make sure you use the correct form of the verb.

anticipate	facilitate	require
comprehend	perceive	terminate
elapse	purchase	undertake

1. He went into the jewellery shop to . . . . a brooch for his wife. (. . . . .)

2. After talking to staff we can . . . . a need for a more efficient method of communicating decisions to the workforce. (. . . . .)

3. A week . . . . before he contacted them again. (. . . . .)

4. Things should be easier now. The law they passed should . . . . the setting up of small businesses. (. . . . .)

5. We shall . . . . more funding if this scheme is to succeed. (. . . . .)

6. If deliveries do not improve, we shall be obliged to . . . . the contract. (. . . . .)

7. We do not . . . . any problems at this stage. (. . . . .)

8. They have . . . . to repay the money by the end of the month. (. . . . .)

9. We feel that the Directors have completely failed to . . . . how unsuitable the site is. (. . . . .)

36 Special areas – 3 Investing

Choose the best alternative to complete each sentence.

1. If a company needs to raise a lot of money, it may . . . . shares.
   a. put up   **b.** issue   **c.** supply   **d.** purchase
2. Pension . . . . play an important role in the stock market.
   a. companies   **b.** trusts   **c.** societies   **d.** funds
3. As an ordinary shareholder, you are . . . . to vote at the meeting.
   a. entitled   **b.** titled   **c.** nominated   **d.** persuaded
4. The share . . . . , which is made up of a cross-section of shares, reflects the general activity of the market.
   a. indication   **b.** index   **c.** measure   **d.** indicator
5. A . . . . is someone who buys shares, expecting the market to rise.
   a. bear   **b.** bull   **c.** dog   **d.** stag
6. A . . . . is a speculator who expects share prices to fall.
   a. bear   **b.** bull   **c.** dog   **d.** stag
7. A . . . . is a person who buys new issues of shares hoping to sell them quickly at a profit.
   a. bear   **b.** bull   **c.** dog   **d.** stag
8. I've put part of the money into an instant . . . . account.
   a. access   **b.** excess   **c.** exit   **d.** entrance
9. Bonds issued by the government are often known as . . . .
   a. golds   **b.** guilts   **c.** gilts   **d.** debits
10. What kind of . . . . can I expect on my investment?
    a. reward   **b.** prize   **c.** surplus   **d.** return
11. You should have as diversified a . . . . of shares as possible.
    a. case   **b.** file   **c.** portfolio   **d.** folder
12. In real . . . . , the $1,000 you invested would be worth $5,000 today.
    a. words   **b.** facts   **c.** factors   **d.** terms
13. The higher the risk you . . . . , the more money you could make.
    a. take   **b.** do   **c.** make   **d.** invest
14. The market has been extremely . . . . over the past few years.
    a. volatile   **b.** wavering   **c.** shocking   **d.** moving

---

A s you did the exercise, did you make a note of these partnerships?

stock market   a return on an investment

Look through the sentences again and underline any other word partnerships you find.

---

37 Social English – 2

Complete each of these conversations with an appropriate response from the list below. Use each response once only.

a. I don't think so.
b. Yes. As a matter of fact, it's my hobby.
c. Reception's as good a place as any.
d. Just a fruit juice, please.
e. Yes we must. I'll look forward to it.
f. I'm afraid not. It was fully booked.
g. Oh you shouldn't have! Thank you!
h. You're welcome.
i. It's difficult to say at this stage.
j. Oh it doesn't matter.
k. Not at all. Go ahead.
l. Do you think you could make it a bit earlier?

1. . . . .

2. . . . .

3. . . . .

4. . . . .

5. . . . .

6. . . . .

7. . . . .

8. . . . .

9. . . . .

10. . . . .

11. . . . .

12. . . . .

38 Applying for a job

I f you have an opportunity to read job advertisements in English, use them to build your vocabulary. Notice especially how certain words and phrases keep recurring. You can also find information about the kinds of things people are expected to do in the jobs advertised.

A.

Below you will see some extracts from job advertisements. Fill in each blank with a word or phrase from the following list. Use each item once only.

attractive	initiative	suit	kitchen staff
ability	outgoing	team	pension scheme
clear	preference	willing	potential customers
contact	required	busy office	successful candidate
experience	skills	hard work	thorough training

Our new 200-seat restaurant is opening in May and we are looking for waiters, waitresses and **1**.........

If you are a friendly and **2**........ person who is not afraid of **3**........, we have the job and hours to **4**........ you.

For more information, **5**........ Helen on 443621.

Typist/Receptionist **6**........ for a **7**........ Typing and shorthand between 80 and 120 wpm. We will give **8**........ to applicants who have experience of using word processors and computers.

TELEPHONE SALES EXECUTIVE

We want a positive person who is **9**........ to work hard and can use their own **10**........ You must be lively and have a good sense of humour and a **11**........ speaking voice.

You will receive **12**........ to enable you to inform **13**........ of the benefits of advertising with us.

Send c.v. to:

ACCOUNTS CLERK

The **14**........ will have had **15**........ of book-keeping and banking procedures.

The position calls for VDU and secretarial **16**........ plus the **17**........ to work as part of a **18**........

An **19**........ salary is offered as well as a company **20**........

B.

Now you will see extracts from two letters about the advertisement for an accounts clerk.
Fill in each blank with a word from the following list. Use each word once only.

as	enclose	form	position
audio	enquiries	further	take
available	favourably	in	to
consider	for	opportunity	with

Dear Sir

With reference 1. . . . . your advertisement in today's 'Morning News', I am interested 2. . . . . applying for the 3. . . . . of accounts clerk with your company.

Could you please send me 4. . . . . details and an application 5. . . . .

Yours faithfully

Dear Sir

I would like to apply 6. . . . . the position of accounts clerk with your company.

I 7. . . . . my application form.

I am at present working 8. . . . . a secretary in the accounts office at TW Industries. My duties include 9. . . . . and copy typing and dealing 10. . . . . correspondence and telephone 11. . . . .

Twice a week I have been going to evening classes in book-keeping and I intend to 12. . . . . an examination in three months.

I am applying for the position because I would like an 13. . . . . to make more use of my training.

I would be 14. . . . . for interview at any time.

I hope that you will 15. . . . . my application 16. . . . .

Yours faithfully

39 Past tense – 2

Remember to check if a verb is irregular when you learn a new one. Remember also that some verbs that end in -ed in their past form have changes in their spelling, for example:

   try   tried   stop   stopped

Complete each of the sentences by using the past form of one of the verbs on the left and combining it with one of the words on the right. Use each verb once only. Some words on the right are used more than once.

bring	give	rely	stick	back	off	over
carry	lay	run	stop	forward	on	to
come	leave	set		in	out	up
draw	pay	stand				

1. We . . . . of computer paper and we had to order some more.

2. They . . . . a survey on biological detergents.

3. He was bankrupt but he . . . . a company in his wife's name.

4. I . . . . for Claire while she was away at the conference.

5. The workers . . . . on strike when the management refused to increase their offer.

6. On the way to Australia I . . . . in Bangkok for two days.

7. They . . . . an agreement which satisfied both sides.

8. They . . . . the meeting . . . . from Friday 7th to Monday 3rd.

9. Unfortunately we . . . . a supplier who was not able to supply us with the components he had promised.

10. They . . . . to consumer pressure and redesigned the packet.

11. In his speech he . . . . the most important detail. How much is it all going to cost?

12. Last year Firmin's . . . . half their workforce because of a lack of orders.

13. He . . . . his original demand. We couldn't get him to change his mind.

14. They . . . . the money they had borrowed only after we had threatened to take them to court.

40 Special areas – 4 Accounting

Choose the best alternative to complete the sentence.

1. It's up to the accountant to . . . . the various financial statements.
   a. interpret   **b.** intercept   **c.** invent   **d.** translate

2. The bookkeeper keeps a record of every financial . . . .
   a. action   **b.** transaction   **c.** entry   **d.** transcription

3. It's essential to . . . . the invoice number in any correspondence.
   a. estimate   **b.** quote   **c.** say   **d.** tell

4. The . . . . of the invoice goes to the customer, another copy goes to Sales, and we keep the other one here in Accounts.
   a. photocopy   **b.** issue   **c.** top copy   **d.** account

5. We're in . . . . with our supplier over this invoice so don't pay it until you hear from me.
   a. argument   **b.** dispute   **c.** agreement   **d.** distress

6. We send a . . . . to customers who haven't settled their accounts.
   a. reminder   **b.** remainder   **c.** remembrance   **d.** memory

7. If these figures could be . . . . into parts and labour it would make them easier to understand.
   a. set up   **b.** broken down   **c.** rounded up   **d.** laid down

8. This company has a weekly . . . . of about £100,000.
   a. pay   **b.** payroll   **c.** salary   **d.** wage

9. Buying that new machinery has seriously . . . . our reserves.
   a. depreciated   **b.** depleted   **c.** depressed   **d.** deprived

10. By examining the balance . . . . and other documents we were able to find out that the company was not doing as well as they claimed.
    a. slip   **b.** ledger   **c.** account   **d.** sheet

11. Surely we can set some off these expenses . . . . tax.
    a. against   **b.** for   **c.** on   **d.** from

12. The rent for the office is already 3 months . . . . !
    a. overtime   **b.** in the red   **c.** in demand   **d.** overdue

13. Due to the economic climate we have had to . . . . more bad debts this year than ever before.
    a. tell off   **b.** write off   **c.** find out   **d.** note down

14. Do they have enough working . . . . to keep trading?
    a. capital   **b.** expenses   **c.** accounts   **d.** currency

15. Such items as buildings and machinery are known as . . . . assets.
    a. current   **b.** hidden   **c.** fixed   **d.** liquid

41 Important adjectives

Spelling is often a problem in English. It is a good idea to make lists of words you find difficult to spell and test yourself regularly on them.
When you have done the exercise below, make two lists with the words and see how many more examples you can think of.

Is an 'a' or an 'e' missing from the following words?

confid nt	depend nt	perman nt
consist nt	domin nt	reluct nt
const nt	effici nt	redund nt
conveni nt	extravag nt	relev nt
curr nt	insolv nt	signific nt

Now complete the following sentences by using one of the adjectives above. Use each adjective once only.

1. I'm . . . . that we'll reach our target without any difficulty.

2. You should be familiar with the regulations . . . . to your work.

3. We must process these orders in a more . . . . way.

4. Unfortunately, the accounts show the company is . . . .

5. Short-term measures aren't enough. We need a more . . . . solution.

6. The advertising campaign had a . . . . effect on their sales.

7. 100 workers were made . . . . when the factory closed.

8. You couldn't get a more . . . . location than next to the station!

9. The figures need . . . . updating as we get more information.

10. I hope interest rates don't stay at the . . . . level much longer!

11. The company fell unexpectedly from its . . . . market position.

12. I wish they had a more . . . . policy on discounts. You never know where you are with them!

13. It was . . . . to spend so much on the press reception.

14. He's . . . . to invest any more money at the moment.

15. We are . . . . on overseas suppliers for most of our components.

42 Word partnerships – 4

Match each adjective on the left with a noun on the right to form common partnerships. Use each word once only. Write your answers in the boxes.

Set 1

1.	continuous	a.	aid
2.	fundamental	b.	brochure
3.	illustrated	c.	control
4.	multi-national	d.	company
5.	potential	e.	customer
6.	prompt	f.	disagreement
7.	strict	g.	reply
8.	visual	h.	supply

1	
2	
3	
4	
5	
6	
7	
8	

Set 2

Now do the same with these words.

1.	advanced	a.	arrangements
2.	alternative	b.	attention
3.	close	c.	expense
4.	competitive	d.	labour
5.	considerable	e.	materials
6.	essential	f.	quote
7.	manual	g.	requirement
8.	raw	h.	technology

1	
2	
3	
4	
5	
6	
7	
8	

Now complete each sentence using a suitable expression from above.

1. We can't use the hall so we'll have to make . . . .

2. They were recently taken over by a . . . .

3. I'd like you to meet her. She could be a . . . .

4. I want you to pay . . . . to everything he does.

43 Special areas – 5 Industrial relations

Choose the best alternative to complete each sentence.

1. Where there was a closed . . . . agreement an employer could not hire non-union workers.
    a. shop   **b.** work   **c.** factory   **d.** business

2. Talks must take place within the . . . . of the national agreement.
    a. network   **b.** contest   **c.** framework   **d.** working party

3. We feel that salaries should at least keep . . . . with inflation.
    a. step   **b.** still   **c.** place   **d.** pace

4. They proposed to minimise the effect of redundancy by relying on natural . . . .
    a. wastage   **b.** waste   **c.** time-wasting   **d.** wasting away

5. With . . . . bargaining the unions negotiate on behalf of groups of workers, not individuals.
    a. collected   **b.** collection   **c.** collective   **d.** collecting

6. Depending on the result of the ballot, they may . . . . a strike.
    a. name   **b.** call   **c.** make   **d.** do

7. If they work to . . . . , the job might not be completed on time.
    a. rule   **b.** order   **c.** rules   **d.** regulation

8. The increase will be . . . . on employees agreeing to a scheme to improve productivity.
    a. linked   **b.** connected   **c.** dependent   **d.** joined

9. Union members were asked not to cross the . . . . line.
    a. boycott   **b.** strike   **c.** picket   **d.** boundary

10. The union seemed powerless to stop the . . . . strikes.
    a. wildcat   **b.** mad dog   **c.** bald eagle   **d.** mad bull

11. The employers tried a . . . . to force the staff to accept their terms.
    a. lock-up   **b.** markup   **c.** lockout   **d.** knock-down

12. We've decided to recommend a half-day . . . . strike in support of our claim.
    a. voucher   **b.** token   **c.** backing   **d.** symbol

13. As we agreed to . . . . arbitration, we'll have to accept the decision.
    a. voluntary   **b.** free   **c.** binding   **d.** party

14. They voted to . . . . and try to prevent the factory from closing.
    a. set out   **b.** sit out   **c.** sit in   **d.** set up

15. As the unions have concentrated on the lower-paid workers in previous negotiations, ... have been eroded.
    a. differences   **b.** definitions   **c.** demonstrations   **d.** differentials

44 In the office – 2

Can you name all the items below? Use each of these words once only.

calculator   paper clips   scales   staples
date stamp   pencil sharpener scissors   string
guillotine   punch   stamps   tray
note pad   ruler   stapler   wastepaper bin

1. . . . .   2. . . . .   3. . . . .   4. . . . .

5. . . . .   6. . . . .   7. . . . .   8. . . . .

9. . . . .   10. . . . .   11. . . . .   12. . . . .

13. . . . .   14. . . . .   15. . . . .   16. . . . .

Now look at the page for one minute and then cover it. See how many items you
can remember.

45 Noun and preposition

Combine a noun from the list on the left with a preposition from the list on the right to complete each sentence. You must use each noun once only, but each preposition can be used more than once.

access	congratulations	increase	result	
admiration	effect	intention	solution	**for in**
chance	emphasis	interest		**of on to**
confidence	experience	point		

1. He was full of . . . . the way she had chaired the meeting.

2. The rise in interest rates has had a considerable . . . . sales of furniture and kitchen appliances.

3. By taking them over we shall gain . . . . new markets.

4. We have every . . . . your organising ability.

5. I hope they find a . . . . this storage problem soon!

6. To cater for the growing . . . . information technology, we have had to put on three extra courses this year.

7. Is there any . . . . seeing you about this some time today?

8. We need to put more . . . . improving staff morale rather than buying more equipment.

9. Have you had any . . . . this type of work?

10. There seemed to be little . . . . continuing the discussion.

11. They have been offered a considerable . . . . salary in return for more flexibility.

12. I have no . . . . resigning. It's up to them to dismiss me if they aren't satisfied.

13. By the way, ... winning the Waverley contract!

14. As a . . . . the adverse publicity, their sales went down.

H ow many of the expressions are followed by the **-ing** form of the verb? Look through the sentences again and underline the **-ing** forms. The examples on this page show again the importance of word partnerships.

---

46 Two-word expressions – 2

Join one word on the left with one from the right to make a two-word partnership. Use each word once only. Write your answers in the boxes.

1. application	**a.** bid	1	
2. assembly	**b.** bonus	2	
3. balance	**c.** book	3	
4. cheque	**d.** buyout	4	
5. consumer	**e.** chart	5	
6. feasibility	**f.** control	6	
7. growth	**g.** form	7	
8. mail	**h.** issue	8	
9. management	**i.** line	9	
10. market	**j.** potential	10	
11. pie	**k.** protection	11	
12. productivity	**l.** research	12	
13. quality	**m.** scale	13	
14. salary	**n.** sheet	14	
15. share	**o.** shot	15	
16. takeover	**p.** study	16	

Now complete each sentence with one of the expressions.

1. If you produce above this amount, you get a . . . .

2. Working on this . . . . every day is very monotonous.

3. A big multi-national has made a . . . . for our company.

4. We carried out extensive . . . . before launching the product.

5. He's at the bottom of the . . . . so how can he afford it?

6. According to the . . . . , they made a large profit last year.

47 What's the job?

In this exercise you will see extracts from job advertisements.

You must decide which job is being referred to in each case.

Choose the job from the following list.

Each job is referred to once only.

Be careful because some of the jobs are looking for similar qualities from applicants.

accountant	clerk	personnel officer
advertising executive	computer operator	R&D Manager
assembly person	draughtsperson	receptionist
chauffeur	motor mechanic	salesperson

You will be in charge of a team of highly creative individuals delivering new quality products and enhancing our existing range.

With particular responsibilities for recruitment and selection. Communication skills and a pragmatic approach to problem solving essential.

1. . . . .

2. . . . .

With mechanical design experience to work as a member of a team producing designs and drawings for production. Experience of our product range is not essential.

Duties include filing, mailing, relief reception and other general office work.

3. . . . .

4. . . . .

Needed for night shift. Clean modern factory. Varied work. Good eyesight essential.

Successful applicant will be articulate and presentable. Remuneration includes retainer and car allowance plus commission structure.

5. . . . .

6. . . . .

Reporting directly to Managing
Director. You will take over
financial control for
all aspects of daily operation.

Sober habits, clean driving
licence, able to be on call 7
days per week at times.
Uniform supplied.

7. . . . .

Must be experienced in the
repair and maintenance of
heavy duty vehicles. References
must be provided from previous
employers.

8. . . . .

You are the first person our
clients will meet so you need
to be friendly, stylish and
efficient.

9. . . . .

Some experience in the
above-mentioned software is
essential but training will be
given to the successful
applicant.

10. . . . .

You will be an essential member
of an agency responsible for
some of the country's top
accounts. You will be
responsible for the
administration of local and
national promotions.

11. . . . .

12. . . . .

A s you were reading the advertisements, did you notice word partnerships
such as *financial control* and *communication skills* ?
Look through the advertisements again and see how many more you can find.

Complete each of the sentences below with a suitable word partnership taken
from the advertisements.

1. We're looking for new products to add to our . . . .

2. She's an . . . . of this team. We can't do without her.

3. You get more money if you work on the . . . . but it ruins your social life.

4. He had a very . . . . to solving problems.

5. I didn't get the job as a driver as I didn't have a . . . .

6. My . . . . are health and safety but I'm also concerned with the general
   welfare of employees.

48 Special areas – 6 Insurance

Choose the best alternative to complete each sentence.

1. Insurance companies can be considered as professional . . . . takers.
   a. life   **b.** risk   **c.** chance   **d.** misfortune

2. Some of the language in insurance . . . . is incomprehensible to most ordinary people.
   a. premiums   **b.** policies   **c.** rates   **d.** invoices

3. The company will . . . . the policy-holder against loss of or damage to the insured vehicle.
   a. identify   **b.** respect   **c.** indemnify   **d.** engage

4. Insurance companies like you to . . . . your claim as soon as possible.
   a. process   **b.** submit   **c.** assure   **d.** proceed

5. Go to an insurance . . . . and see if you can get a better deal.
   a. breaker   **b.** broker   **c.** speculator   **d.** merchant

6. In these inflationary times it is important to keep the value of your policy closely . . . . to the value of your property.
   a. adapted   **b.** linked   **c.** indicated   **d.** dependent

7. My insurance company offers a wide . . . . of cover.
   a. range   **b.** branch   **c.** rank   **d.** standard

8. His insurance company had told him not to admit . . . . , even though it was clearly his fault.
   a. legality   **b.** likelihood   **c.** liability   **d.** crime

9. My endowment policy will . . . . when I'm sixty-five.
   a. ripen   **b.** mature   **c.** flourish   **d.** break

10. . . . . insurance originated in the fifteenth century.
    a. Boat   **b.** Sea   **c.** Navy   **d.** Marine

11. The . . . . form you fill in is the basis of your contract with the insurance company.
    a. proposition   **b.** application   **c.** enrolment   **d.** proposal

12. The insurance will be . . . . if you omit any relevant information.
    a. void   **b.** valid   **c.** invaluable   **d.** priceless

13. You're allowed 30 days' . . . . for the payment of the renewal premium.
    a. grace   **b.** favour   **c.** way   **d.** permission

14. Make sure all this equipment is insured . . . . accidental damage.
    a. over   **b.** against   **c.** with   **d.** from

49 Expressions with 'take'

Complete each sentence with the correct form of 'take' and a word from the list below. Use each word once only.

call	down	on	seriously
chair	further	out	steps
charge	home	over	up
consideration	off	risk	

1. You should . . . . an additional policy covering you against accidental damage.

2. We had to . . . . extra staff during the holiday season.

3. When all the transport costs have been . . . . into . . . . , we have in fact made a loss.

4. Sales really . . . . after the product had been mentioned on television.

5. A good sales rep can . . . . over £500 a week.

6. If my phone rings, could you . . . . the . . . . for me?

7. We must . . . . to see that we don't lose our market share as a result of this increased competition.

8. If the boss is ill, who'll . . . . the . . . . at the meeting?

9. He didn't seem to . . . . the threat of redundancy very . . . .

10. Don't . . . . this . . . . , Angela. I'm just thinking aloud.

11. In 1988 we were . . . . by a large multi-national company.

12. If the account is not settled within seven days, we shall be obliged to . . . . the matter . . . .

13. Mrs Jenkins has been appointed to . . . . of our Canterbury branch.

14. I'm not sure if there is a market for this kind of product but you don't get anywhere without . . . . a . . . . now and again.

15. They decided not to . . . . the option, so we had to look around for other potential purchasers.

N otice once again how important word partnerships are. Underline all the expressions using 'take' and other words.

---

50 Colourful language

Many journalists who write about business like to use idiomatic expressions to make what they say more interesting to the reader.
As some of these expressions occur regularly, it is important to understand them and note them down.

Complete each of the sentences with one of the words or phrases below. Use each item once only.

carry the can	**on the grapevine**	**thorny problem**
a dawn raid	**ride rough-shod**	**type-cast**
fall by the wayside	**ride the storm**	**undermine**
hefty knock	**rubber-stamp**	**wiped off**
nose-dive	**teething problems**	**woo**

1. They attempt to . . . . the housewife with special offers.

2. Despite . . . . in the first few months, the new system has proved to be a great success.

3. He then turned to the . . . . of appraisal interviews, a topic which he knew would be unpopular.

4. If you . . . . over your opponents you should not be surprised if they take every opportunity to get their revenge.

5. She accuses some of the directors of trying to . . . . her position in the company.

6. They had heard . . . . that he was thinking of leaving.

7. They were left to . . . . after the firm collapsed.

8. Luckily we were able to . . . . until things had calmed down.

9. The pound took a . . . . yesterday when the trade figures turned out to be much worse than anyone had expected.

10. Over £17 million was . . . . the value of the company after it was announced that they had made a substantial loss.

11. She's been . . . . as a risk-taker but in fact she's usually a very cautious person.

12. The committee did little more than . . . . the new policy.

13. Inevitably many new products . . . . in the rush for profits.

14. They gained control of the company after . . . . that caught the directors and the stock market completely by surprise.

15. The bad news caused the shares to . . . . 65p to 85p.

51 Confusing words – 2

Choose the correct word for each sentence.

1. I'll ask my bank manager for **advice/ advise** about investment.

2. He first spoke **briefly/shortly** about the agenda for the day.

3. She hopes to get a **chair/seat** on the board.

4. We **check/control** each new consignment very carefully.

5. I enclosed a **complements/compliments** slip with the catalogue.

6. Do these cars **confirm/conform** to the new safety regulations?

7. You shouldn't read **confident/confidential** documents!

8. Normally, she's a very **conscientious/conscious** worker.

9. The unions criticised the government's **economic/economical** policy.

10. If you pay too much tax you get a **discount/rebate**.

11. Lawyers here only get their **fee/wages** if they win the case.

12. The **income/salary** from the investment is £52,000 a year.

13. She took her case to an **industrial/industrious** tribunal.

14. Unfortunately we have **mislaid/misled** the original invoice.

15. The secretary made **notes/notices** of what was said at the meeting.

16. The **overtake/takeover** bid from Jenkins came as a complete surprise.

17. Please send me your latest catalogue and **price/prize** list.

18. We've increased **produce/productivity** by 10% in this factory.

N ow see if you can write a new, correct sentence using the incorrect word from each of these sentences. This will help you to remember how to use the words you have seen.

---

52 Word formation – 3

Remember to keep looking for words that are formed from the same basic word. Make lists of these words and test yourself. Try to use the words in sentences. This will help you to remember them.

Complete each sentence with the correct form of the word in capital letters. In some cases you will have to make a negative form by using the prefix **dis-** or **un-**.

1. MANAGE
Since the . . . . buy-out profits have risen sharply.

The . . . . Director sent a letter to every member of staff.

It makes sense to break the task up into . . . . steps.

2. NEGOTIATE
The salary is . . . . so how much do you think I should ask for?

Unfortunately, ... with the union have broken down.

3. OCCUPY
The block has been . . . . since the fire.

Dust is an . . . . hazard in this factory.

4. OPERATE
The oil rig should be in . . . . by tomorrow morning.

We expect an . . . . profit of at least 20 million francs next year.

The scheme should be fully . . . . by this time next year.

The switchboard . . . . was unable to find the person I wanted.

5. OPT
Although insurance is . . . . , we strongly recommend it.

I want to leave my . . . . open, so I haven't given him my answer yet.

6. ORIGIN
We . . . . intended to close only three of our branches.

The idea is said to have . . . . from the Sales Department.

Her proposal showed a lot of . . . . - perhaps too much, in fact.

7. PREFER
We'll obviously give . . . . to candidates with previous experience.

They gave her the loan at a . . . . rate of interest.

8. PRODUCE

The new model should be in . . . . in three months.
The finished . . . . must leave the factory in perfect condition.
I'm afraid our talks with the manufacturers have been . . . .
Any . . . . bonus will be paid every 4 months.

9. PROFIT

Any line which proved . . . . was immediately discontinued.
Couldn't some workers be more . . . . employed in other departments?
Doubts have been expressed as to the . . . . of the business.

10. RESTRICT

They have imposed . . . . on the sales of certain electronic goods.
Such . . . . trade practices are not in the public interest.
I'm afraid access to this information is . . . .

11. SATISFY

What job . . . . can anybody get from working on an assembly line?
We hope the discussions with our creditors will have a . . . . outcome.
The customer was . . . . with the service and complained to the boss.

12. SYSTEM

You need to have a . . . . approach in this type of work.
We need to carry out this survey . . . .

13. SUIT

I'm not sure about the . . . . of the site for the new factory.
We now have to find a . . . . name for our new chocolate bar.

14. VARY

Our company produces a great . . . . of toys.
Remember the interest rate is . . . . , so you could have problems.
They put forward . . . . suggestions but none was acceptable.

O ften the words are used as parts of word partnerships, for example:

give preference   **job satisfaction**

Underline other useful partnerships you can find in the sentences.

---

53 Special areas – 7 International trade

Choose the best alternative to complete the sentence.

1. Many countries, such as the United Kingdom and New Zealand, are . . . . dependent on international trade.
   a. favourably   **b.** heavily   **c.** perfectly   **d.** grossly

2. The fact that labour costs are lower in other countries . . . . us at a tremendous disadvantage.
   a. makes   **b.** does   **c.** puts   **d.** sells

3. If a country has a . . . . currency, importers and exporters may have to keep changing the prices of their goods.
   a. swimming   **b.** flying   **c.** flowing   **d.** floating

4. Some countries try to be . . . . in certain commodities so that they are not dependent on imports.
   a. economic   **b.** sufficient   **c.** self-sufficient   **d.** self-financing

5. It's better to start exporting on a small . . . . and then expand if things go well.
   a. measure   **b.** measurement   **c.** scale   **d.** rate

6. Because of high shipping costs, it made more sense to . . . . a manufacturer to produce our range of furniture.
   a. license   **b.** lease   **c.** control   **d.** handle

7. The government has imposed protective tariffs to stop the . . . . of cheap imports which threatened to destroy domestic industries.
   a. rain   **b.** famine   **c.** flood   **d.** storm

8. Some manufacturers were accused of . . . . , in other words selling goods abroad at a lower price than they were sold domestically.
   a. dumping   **b.** revaluing   **c.** flooding   **d.** devaluation

9. Employing more staff has reduced our . . . . time in the port.
   a. turning   **b.** turn-round   **c.** turn back   **d.** turnover

10. The technical . . . . for electrical equipment can vary from country to country.
    a. justification   **b.** rules   **c.** specifications   **d.** uniforms

11. Many goods coming here are subject . . . . customs duty.
    a. for   **b.** to   **c.** of   **d.** with

12. Among other things, a . . . . contains details of the goods, their destination and the name of the ship carrying them.
    a. bill of lading   **b.** way-bill   **c.** bill of exchange   **d.** receipt

13. The person the goods are sent to is called a . . . .
    a. consignor   **b.** consignee   **c.** commissioner   **d.** master

14. She looked at the . . . . to check where the goods were produced.
    a. certificate of origin   **b.** test certificate   **c.** postmark   **d.** trade mark

15. Because of the recession, several ships have been laid . . . .
    a. off   **b.** out   **c.** down   **d.** up

54 Colour idioms

Complete each sentence with the correct colour.

1. His supervisor gave him a . . . . look when he turned up late for the third time this week.

2. I must be on some kind of . . . . list because I have a lot of difficulty getting credit.

3. We're waiting for the . . . . light from head office to launch our publicity campaign.

4. Local residents protested when they heard a factory was going to be built in a . . . . belt area.

5. I won't believe we've got the contract until I see it down in . . . . and . . . .

6. Among the . . . . goods, washing machines are our best sellers.

7. There were several . . . . faces when these so-called financial experts found that they had been tricked!

8. We need to cut through all the . . . . tape and speed up the decision-making process.

9. That's a bit of a . . . . area. It's difficult to say who exactly has responsibility for recruitment.

10. The company found itself several thousand pounds in the . . . . after spending so much on improving its production line.

11. We lose millions in tax revenue every year because of the . . . . economy.

12. They're looking for a . . . . knight to help them fight the takeover bid.

13. Then, out of the . . . . , she offered me a job managing her new restaurant. You can imagine my surprise.

14. We have to roll out the . . . . carpet for him as he's one of our best customers.

15. The . . . . revolution has meant that food exports have increased dramatically in the past few years.

16. The Government intends to allocate more money to unemployment . . . . spots.

71

55 Adjective and preposition

Combine an adjective from the list on the left with a preposition from the list on the right to complete each sentence. You must use each adjective once only, but each preposition can be used more than once.

acceptable	capable	eligible	proud		
accustomed	consistent	envious	relevant	**for**	**of**
available	contrary	familiar	responsible	**on**	**to** **with**
aware	dependent	popular	well-known		

1. I'm sure they must be . . . . our products as they're used all over the world.

2. If you pay within seven days you will be . . . . a discount.

3. I will be . . . . interview at any time.

4. The other salespeople were all . . . . her success and so they were pleased when she left.

5. . . . . expectations, our sales figures went down last month.

6. Our new range of toys has proved very . . . . children who have watched the television programme.

7. Any decisions made must be . . . . the company's overall marketing strategy.

8. The maintenance engineer is . . . . checking every machine at least once a week.

9. I'm not . . . . any regulations that should prevent us from exporting to those countries.

10. We need somebody who is . . . . understanding German.

11. That's an interesting point but it isn't really . . . . our discussion.

12. It took me some time to become . . . . using the new system.

13. They will only sign if the terms are fully . . . . them.

14. It's risky to be . . . . only one supplier.

15. He was so . . . . his firm's achievements that he talked about them to everyone he met.

16. This company is . . . . the high quality of its products.

56 Word partnerships – 5

Match each verb on the left with a noun on the right to form common partnerships. Use each word once only. Write your answers in the boxes.

Set 1

1. attend	**a.** a compromise		1	
2. consult	**b.** a conference		2	
3. establish	**c.** an error		3	
4. issue	**d.** funds		4	
5. reach	**e.** instructions		5	
6. rectify	**f.** a lawyer		6	
7. subsidise	**g.** priorities		7	
8. transfer	**h.** the staff canteen		8	

Set 2

Now do the same with these words.

1. allocate	**a.** a deal		1	
2. break	**b.** a demand		2	
3. clinch	**c.** duty		3	
4. corner	**d.** figures		4	
5. meet	**e.** the market		5	
6. pay	**f.** new ground		6	
7. raise	**g.** standards		7	
8. update	**h.** tasks		8	

Now complete each sentence using a suitable expression from above.

1. They . . . . so the food's not too expensive.

2. I had to . . . . on those items when I came through customs.

3. If they're threatening to take you to court you'd better . . . .

4. How easy is it to . . . . to a bank in another country?

73

57 Special areas – 8 Personnel

Choose the best alternative to complete each sentence.

1. The personnel department . . . . a job analysis, which is a detailed study of the elements and characteristics of each job.
    a. carries on   **b.** carries out   **c.** goes on   **d.** goes through

2. They write a job description specifying the . . . . of the job.
    a. objects   **b.** objectives   **c.** results   **d.** characters

3. You should encourage employees . . . . openly about any problems.
    a. for speaking   **b.** to tell   **c.** to say   **d.** to speak.

4. The first step in the disciplinary procedure is an . . . . reprimand.
    a. aural   **b.** oral   **c.** open   **d.** overt

5. She doesn't seem to . . . . very well with the other secretaries.
    a. come on   **b.** get on   **c.** get by   **d.** get through

6. By organising job . . . . you can give staff experience in many different departments.
    a. revolution   **b.** recycling   **c.** circulation   **d.** rotation

7. After . . . . our training programme, we made some changes.
    a. evaluating   **b.** valuing   **c.** vindicating   **d.** validating

8. Our selection procedure is based on the old saying: "You can't fit a square . . . . into a round hole."
    a. bar   **b.** stick   **c.** wood   **d.** peg

9. Before you get the job you have to have a . . . . examination.
    a. medicine   **b.** mechanical   **c.** medical   **d.** medicinal

10. Training new staff is . . . . , so you must pick the right person.
    a. costly   **b.** priceless   **c.** valuable   **d.** cost-effective

11. We can't use . . . . titles such as 'postman' and 'fireman'.
    a. sexual   **b.** sexy   **c.** sexist   **d.** sexism

12. We have a policy of . . . . our own employees first for any vacancies.
    a. thinking   **b.** considering   **c.** asking   **d.** telling

13. As part of the . . . . process, Personnel check each applicant's qualifications before considering them for interview.
    a. monitoring   **b.** warning   **c.** screening   **d.** forecasting

14. Tests are used to measure the applicant's . . . . for the job.
    a. attitude   **b.** success   **c.** discrimination   **d.** aptitude

15. The personnel department helps to organise an . . . . programme for each new employee.
    a. orientation   **b.** orienteering   **c.** inducement   **d.** endurance

16. If we have to dismiss an employee this means the . . . . process has failed in some way.
    a. selective   **b.** chosen   **c.** selection   **d.** choice

17. Highly-skilled jobs are usually advertised in the . . . . media, such as technical magazines.
    a. special   **b.** speciality   **c.** specialist   **d.** specialisation

18. Using a standardised application form ensures we get all the . . . . we need.
    a. particulars   **b.** specialities   **c.** peculiarities   **d.** experience

19. One important aspect of welfare is ensuring that there is no . . . . in the work place.
    a. discrepancy   **b.** harmony   **c.** discrimination   **d.** discretion

20. Some of the employees were not happy about the introduction of a yearly . . . . interview.
    a. approval   **b.** appraisal   **c.** appreciation   **d.** appropriation

21. Her work was beginning to suffer because of family . . . .
    a. committees   **b.** commissions   **c.** competition   **d.** commitments

22. After a time employees may feel they are . . . . with a job they find tedious.
    a. glued   **b.** stuck   ᵢastened   **d.** attached

23. His work is generally satisfactory ᵥ ᵤt unfortunately he has a . . . . against his supervisor.
    a. hatred   **b.** dissatisfaction   **c.** disagreement   **d.** grudge

24. "Why does the personnel manager always . . . . me? I'm not the only one who comes late!"
    a. pick up   **b.** pick on   **c.** pick with   **d.** pick out

25. In cases of . . . . we sometimes make loans to employees.
    a. hard cash   **b.** hardship   **c.** hard labour   **d.** hard sell.

26. In R & D, for example, employing someone . . . . unorthodox may produce stimulating ideas.
    a. slightly   **b.** scarcely   **c.** lightly   **d.** hardly

27. A complete . . . . is kept on every senior member of staff from the moment they are appointed.
    a. document   **b.** paper   **c.** dossier   **d.** diary

28. Positive . . . . is essential so that staff know that their efforts are appreciated.
    a. feedback   **b.** discrimination   **c.** commentary   **d.** notification

58 Expressions with 'in'

Remember to keep looking for examples of words which combine together to form common expressions.

There are several expressions in English using prepositions. If you look up one of these expressions in a dictionary you will sometimes find it under the preposition. Often, however, you have to look under the noun.

Here are some expressions with 'in'. Make sure you understand them before doing the exercise.

in accordance with	in debt	in the process of
in advance	in due course	in round figures
in arrears	in error	in stock
in circulation	in a position to	in transit

Put the correct expression from the above list into the following sentences. Use each expression once only.

1. We regret that we are not . . . . extend you any more credit.

2. We have sold your car . . . . your instructions.

3. The government wants to reduce the amount of money . . . .

4. He is heavily . . . . because he still hasn't been paid for the last job he did.

5. . . . . it was £8,000 – the exact figure was £7,985.

6. You'll receive half the payment . . . . and the rest when the work has been completed.

7. We have over 500 carpets . . . . in our warehouse.

8. The goods were sent . . . . We apologise for any inconvenience this may have caused.

9. You should receive the information . . . . so please try and be patient.

10. They are . . . . installing a new computer-controlled system, so your order might be delayed.

11. They took him to court because he was 14 months . . . . with the rent.

12. The goods were damaged . . . . from the factory to the warehouse.

59 Advertising – 2

Choose the best alternative to complete the sentence.
Look up any words you don't know.

1. With effective advertising a company can become a . . . . name.
   a. house   **b.** household   **c.** housewife's   **d.** home

2. We need an effective campaign to . . . . our new product range.
   a. fire   **b.** set out   **c.** set off   **d.** launch

3. During the commercial . . . . , there was an advertisement for a new women's magazine.
   a. break   **b.** breakage   **c.** pause   **d.** interval

4. The first thing an ad must do is . . . . the reader's eye.
   a. trap   **b.** catch   **c.** find   **d.** reach

5. We need a name for the product which will . . . . to teenagers.
   a. draw   **b.** attract   **c.** succeed   **d.** appeal

6. They decided to do a mail . . . . to get people interested in their holiday homes.
   a. shot   **b.** shoot   **c.** trial   **d.** list

7. All advertisers must obey the industry's . . . .
   a. practice code   **b.** code of practice   **c.** practical code   **d.** code word

8. Advertising on television is very expensive during . . . . viewing hours.
   a. peak   **b.** high   **c.** audience   **d.** big

9. We did a lot of research to ensure that the advertisement would appeal to the . . . . audience.
   a. aim   **b.** arrival   **c.** goal   **d.** target

10. Newspaper advertising . . . . for 45% of the total.
    a. accounted   **b.** counted   **c.** comprised   **d.** came

11. Advertisers look at each newspaper's . . . . figures before deciding where to place their advertisements.
    a. circular   **b.** population   **c.** circulation   **d.** revenue

12. As part of our service we provide . . . . display material.
    a. selling point   **b.** point-of-sale   **c.** appointed   **d.** salesmanship

13. If you advertise at airports, you have a . . . . audience.
    a. captured   **b.** slave   **c.** captivated   **d.** captive

14. She does the art work while I write the . . . . for each advertisement.
    a. copy   **b.** copies   **c.** copyright   **d.** media

60 Letters – 6
Exhibition information

Below you will see an extract from a letter giving information about a business exhibition. Fill in each blank by using a word or phrase from the list below. Use each item once only.

emphasis	enclosed map	company details	complimentary tickets
enter	great pleasure	comprehensive range	conveniently situated
field	look forward	ideal opportunity	in-depth discussion
speakers	up to date	new feature	series of lectures

We have 1......... in enclosing two 2......... for this year's Business Scene Exhibition.

As your business grows it is important to keep 3......... with the latest developments. With over 400 exhibitors this year the Exhibition is bigger and better than ever. This is the 4......... to see a 5......... of the latest products, services and publications.

A 6......... of the Exhibition this year is a 7......... on international trade and investment. Distinguished 8......... from around the world will give their views on the changes taking place. Special 9......... will be given to the ever-increasing role of the new technologies especially in the 10......... of international communications.

At the end of each lecture there will be opportunities for 11......... of the issues raised.

As you will see from the 12........., the Exhibition takes place at a venue 13......... only a few minutes' walk from the station.

The Exhibition is open from 10 a.m to 6 p.m. on 1st, 2nd and 3rd May.

Simply 14......... your names and 15......... on the badges provided and bring your tickets to the business show of the year!

We 16......... to seeing you there.

61 Word partnerships – 6

A s you use English in business you meet several expressions using 'of', for example:

brand of soap   **exchange of contracts**

Can you think of any more?

In this exercise you must complete the expression on the left by using one of the words on the right. Use each word once only. Write your answer in the space provided.

1. breach	of	absence
2. code	of	charges
3. flag	of	contract
4. leave	of	convenience
5. loss	of	earnings
6. margin	of	embarkation
7. period	of	error
8. port	of	hands
9. rate	of	living
10. scale	of	notice
11. show	of	practice
12. standard	of	return

Now complete the following by using an expression from above.

1. She looked for an investment with a better . . . .

2. The ship sails under a . . . . to save money.

3. They sued him for . . . . as the work was not completed on time.

4. The meeting approved the motion by a . . . .

5. In theory, public relations officers follow a strict . . . .

62 Social English – 3

Match the sentence on the left with a suitable response on the right. Use each sentence once only.

1. And what line of work are you in?

    a. No. This is my first visit, in fact.

2. I'm afraid I haven't brought the letter.

    b. At this time of day? Not very good, I'm afraid.

3. Best of luck on Friday.

    c. Smart move!

4. Shall I get you a taxi?

    d. We've enjoyed having you.

5. How was the conference?

    e. Thanks! We'll need it!

6. What are the chances of finding him at home?

    f. Shall we say about eleven thirty, then?

7. Do you know Chicago at all, Wendy?

    g. I might have. I'll look in my diary.

8. I've decided to look around for a better job.

    h. Public relations.

9. Thursday morning would suit me fine.

    i. Never mind. You can give it to me tomorrow.

10. You haven't got his phone number by any chance?

    j. No, it's all right, thanks. The walk will do me good.

11. How's their recruitment drive going?

    k. Not too bad. I made some useful contacts.

12. It's been very kind of you to put me up.

    l. They've had quite a good response so far.

Write your answers here:

1	2	3	4	5	6	7	8	9	10	11	12

Can you think of any more responses you could give to the sentences on the left?

63 Special areas – 9 The law

Choose the best alternative to complete each sentence.

1. The company took out an . . . . to prevent the newspaper from
    publishing the story.
    a. incentive   **b.** injunction   **c.** inducement   **d.** induction

2. Every business must operate within the legal . . . . of the country.
    a. pattern   **b.** standard   **c.** framework   **d.** requirement

3. They have changed the wording on the packing to . . . . the new
    regulations.
    a. comply with   **b.** come to   **c.** call up   **d.** take up

4. An employer is not allowed to discriminate . . . . an employee because of
    race or colour.
    a. for   **b.** between   **c.** with   **d.** against

5. You realise that you will be . . . . for any debts incurred if you sign this
    agreement?
    a. likely   **b.** apt   **c.** liable   **d.** bound

6. If you fail to deliver on time you will be in . . . . of contract.
    a. break   **b.** failure   **c.** fault   **d.** breach

7. The company threatened to . . . . the newspaper for libel unless an
    immediate apology was published.
    a. court   **b.** sue   **c.** subject   **d.** slander

8. Until you can prove you have a legal . . . . to the property, we are not
    prepared to do business with you.
    a. claim   **b.** responsibility   **c.** action   **d.** status

9. As this is the first case of its kind it really depends on how the
    court . . . . the law.
    a. interprets   **b.** translates   **c.** explains   **d.** performs

10. They proved that the accident was the result of his . . . .
    a. negligent   **b.** responsibility   **c.** negligence   **d.** competence

11. They paid £1 million in . . . . because of those faulty components.
    a. damage   **b.** compensation   **c.** harm   **d.** errors

12. We can't use that name because it's a registered . . . .
    a. trademark   **b.** patent   **c.** logo   **d.** copyright

13. I think we should . . . . our lawyers before signing any agreement.
    a. confirm   **b.** contract   **c.** consign   **d.** consult

14. The new law will strengthen . . . . against unfair dismissal.
    a. safeguards   **b.** prevention   **c.** grants   **d.** avoidance

15. Litigation is on the . . . . as consumers become more conscious of their
    rights.
    a. surge   **b.** escalation   **c.** development   **d.** rise

64 Choose the adverb – 2

From the following list choose a suitable adverb to complete each sentence. Use each adverb once only.

absolutely	**firmly**	**instantaneously**	**unpredictably**
adversely	**formally**	**irretrievably**	**wholly**
consistently	**highly**	**readily**	
convincingly	**initially**	**systematically**	

1. The change-over must be carried out . . . . , one step at a time.

2. Spare parts are . . . . available so there should be no problem.

3. They are a . . . . owned subsidiary of Martin Industries.

4. They have . . . . out-performed their competitors and we see no reason why this should change.

5. Moves are under way to . . . . wind up the company.

6. Are you . . . . certain the appointment was for midday?

7. I . . . . believe that this range will be a winner.

8. Their latest figures demonstrate . . . . that their shares are ready for a big rise! Buy now!

9. I'm afraid talks with the unions have broken down . . . .

10. We've decided to concentrate . . . . on the South Pacific and then, if successful, try to get into other markets.

11. News of the loss could . . . . affect the share price.

12. Electronic mail systems allow you to reply . . . . to messages.

13. The managing director made a . . . . entertaining speech.

14. The markets tend to act . . . . in times of crisis.

N ow look for and underline the word partnerships containing these important adverbs.

---

65 Letters – 7
Booking a hotel room

Below you will see parts of two letters concerned with booking hotel rooms for a company. Put the correct word or phrase in each blank. Choose from the following list. Use each item once only.

available	meet	reasonable rates	suitable
brochure	pleasure	require	training sessions
full board	provide	requirements	urge
hesitate	quotation	single	without delay

A.

We intend to hold **1.** . . . . for our sales representatives at the end of May next year and are looking for a hotel which provides **2.** . . . . facilities.

Our **3.** . . . . are as follows:

    1 room for lectures capable of seating approximately 50 people

    5 smaller rooms for seminars capable of seating 10-12 people

    50-60 **4.** . . . . rooms with bath

If you can **5.** . . . . these facilities, we would be pleased to receive your **6.** . . . . for 3 nights **7.** . . . . starting with dinner on Tuesday and finishing with lunch on Friday.

We look forward to hearing from you.

B.

Thank you for your letter of 6th September, inquiring about our conference facilities.

I have enclosed our **8.** . . . . and price list.

As you will see, we should be able to **9.** . . . . your requirements at what we consider to be very **10.** . . . .

At the moment our rooms are still **11.** . . . . for the end of May, but I would **12.** . . . . you to make your reservation **13.** . . . . as this is a popular time of the year with many companies.

If you **14.** . . . . any further information, please do not **15.** . . . . to contact me.

I hope that we shall have the **16.** . . . . of welcoming you to our hotel.

66 Increasing efficiency

In what ways can an organisation be made more efficient? Before you do this exercise see if you can write down in English at least 5 ways. As you read the text, see if any points are the same as yours.

Remember that predicting what somebody is going to say or write can help you to practise and build your vocabulary.

Fill each blank with the correct word partnership from the list below. Use each partnership once only.

put off unpleasant tasks   **lose concentration**   **separate folders**
delegate routine tasks   **set a time limit**   **set priorities**
unnecessary paperwork   **members of staff**   **skip over**
time-consuming way   **have a meeting**   **pick out**

Here are ten key ways to improve efficiency:

Avoid **1.** . . . . Be ruthless. Are all those statistics and memos really necessary?

Essential paperwork should be organised into **2.** . . . . so that you and other **3.** . . . . can find what you want quickly.

4. . . . . Decide which of your tasks are the most important and deal with them first.

Never **5.** . . . . It is best to deal with them as soon as possible or you will keep thinking about them and **6.** . . . .

Know when to stop. If you are too much of a perfectionist, you will concentrate on one task and not leave enough time to do the others.

7. . . . . Don't try to do everything yourself. Make sure, however, that the subordinate is competent enough to carry out the task.

Cut meetings to a minimum. Ask yourself if a meeting is essential or if the issues could be dealt with in a less **8.** . . . .

If you must **9.** . . . . , restrict it to those whose presence is essential. Don't waste people's time.

At the beginning of a meeting **10.** . . . . and stick to it. This should concentrate everbody's mind and avoid unnecessary anecdotes etc.

Learn the art of speed-reading. **11.** . . . . the non-essential text and **12.** . . . . the message, the important facts.

67 Special areas – 10
Management

Choose the best alternative to complete each sentence.

1. You must keep staff . . . ., especially when things get difficult.
   a. generated   **b.** motivated   **c.** frustrated   **d.** electrified

2. Weigh up the . . . . of each alternative before deciding.
   a. checks and balances   **b.** assets   **c.** pros and cons   **d.** profits

3. A good manager must be able to handle . . . . situations.
   a. sensible   **b.** impressive   **c.** touching   **d.** touchy

4. He decided to let things . . . ., so he dropped the subject until later.
   a. freeze   **b.** ice over   **c.** cool down   **d.** flare up

5. She . . . . creating a better atmosphere amongst the staff.
   a. set about   **b.** set off   **c.** set out   **d.** set down

6. We need to have . . . . arrangements in case things don't work out.
   a. container   **b.** contingency   **c.** consolidated   **d.** consecutive

7. In a meeting you must stop people talking at . . . . purposes.
   a. opposite   **b.** angry   **c.** cross   **d.** opposing

8. Why doesn't he stick to the point? He's always going off . . . .
   a. at an angle   **b.** at a tangent   **c.** by the way   **d.** on the side

9. It's always difficult when a team is working . . . . a deadline.
   a. in   **b.** at   **c.** to   **d.** opposite

10. Try to ensure that each employee's . . . . is not too great.
    a. workload   **b.** working practice   **c.** work-to-rule   **d.** working party

11. Those who can't manage their time efficiently always have high
    stress . . . .
    a. grades   **b.** standards   **c.** performances   **d.** levels

12. The more responsibilities she . . . ., the more mistakes she made.
    a. took off   **b.** took on   **c.** took down   **d.** took out

13. I hope the project continues to run as . . . . as it has so far.
    a. calmly   **b.** confidently   **c.** smoothly   **d.** wisely

14. After . . . . many unforeseen obstacles they just managed to meet their
    deadline.
    a. overtaking   **b.** overcoming   **c.** overwhelming   **d.** overriding

15. What can we do to improve . . . . in this department?
    a. morale   **b.** mortality   **c.** moral   **d.** temperament

As usual, look for and underline useful word partnerships.

Answers

1   1.draft 2.answer the phone, attend a conference, cash a cheque, join a team, program a computer 3.competitors, competition, competitive, competitively 4.drew, led, rose, spread 5.approximately, Company, kilogram(me), FREE ON BOARD (sometimes written f.o.b.), Post Office Box 6.gone, gear, food, height

2   1.campaign, classified ad., commercial, poster 2.check in, reservation, room service, weekend rate 3.apply for, interview, overtime, training, 4.agenda, A.G.M., chairperson, minutes 5.exchange rate, owe, profit, refund 6.fax, filing cabinet, stapler, telex

3   1.calendar 2.filing cabinet 3.umbrella 4.VDU 5.printer 6.files 7.phone 8.keyboard 9.diary 10.passport 11.vase 12.rubber (eraser) 13.pen 14.pencil 15.map 16.cheque book

4   1.Dear 2.advertisement 3.current issue 4.latest catalogue 5.price list 6.forward 7.faithfully 8.reference 9.information 10.particularly 11.model 12.still available 13.advise 14.payment 15.discount 16.price range

5   Set 1 1.e 2.d 3.c 4.a 5.g 6.f 7.b 8.h Set 2 1.h 2.a 3.d 4.e 5.f 6.b 7.g 8.c 1.offer a discount 2.export goods 3.pay tax 4.arrange a meeting

6   1.cut ... off 2.found out 3.kept ... down 4.dealt with 5.read ... back 6.put forward 7.thought ... over 8.got through/on 9.built ... up 10.broke down 11.sold out 12.shut down 13.went on 14.rang back/up 15.took off 16.heard from

7   1.c 2.d 3.j 4.i 5.b 6.k 7.l 8.h 9.a 10.f 11.g 12.e 1.industrial espionage 2.book a flight 3.settled their accounts 4.launch a new product 5.out to dinner

8   1.advertising 2.affect 3.lend 4.postpone 5.inspected 6.delayed 7.economics 8.interested 9.job 10.journey 11.living 12.measurements 13.rise 14.receipt 15.remind 16.tell 17.sensitive 18.stationery

9   1.withdraw 2.cash dispenser 3.issued 4.debited 5.credit rating 6.financial institutions 7.commission 8.statement 9.in full 10.interest 11.outstanding 12.standing order 13.credit transfer 14.slip 15.salaries 16.banker's draft (also called a bank draft)

10   1.e 2.i 3.a 4.j 5.l 6.b 7.k 8.c 9.h 10.d 11.g 12.f

11   1.enquiry 2.pleasure 3.further details 4.hesitate 5.sincerely 6.full details 7.supply 8.enquiring 9.in production 10.enclosed leaflet 11.additional features 12.competitive price 13.range 14.In addition 15.date 16.doing business

12 1.h 2.f 3.m 4.d 5.k 6.c 7.n 8.i 9.l 10.b 11.a 12.g 13.e 14.o 15.j 1.word processor 2.office block 3.exchange rate 4.job satisfaction

13 1.laser printer 2.answer phone 3.burglar alarm 4.cordless phone 5.fax machine 6.computer 7.diary 8.office chair 9.partitioning 10.photocopier 11.signmaking kit 12.clock 13.briefcase 14.pocket calculator 15.pen 16.table lamp

14 1.unacceptable, acceptance 2.action, active, activity 3.additions, additional 4.analysis, analysts 5.applicant, application, applicable 6.assistance, assistant 7.attractions, attractive 8.commercial, commercially, commercialised/ized, commercials 9.connecting, connection, connections 10.contractor, contractually 11.directions, directors, directory, directly, directive 12.indecisive, decision 13.difference, different, differ 14.distributor, distribution 15.economise/ize, economists

15 1.partial 2.approximate 3.internal 4.low 5.light 6.short 7.compulsory 8.full-time 9.negative 10.private 11.complex 12.marked 13.basic 14.permanent

16 Set 1 1.a 2.h 3.b 4.e 5.g 6.f 7.d 8.c Set 2 1.a 2.b 3.e 4.d 5.h 6.c 7.f 8.g 1.introductory offer 2.annual conference 3.early retirement 4.skilled workers

17 1.c 2.e 3.g 4.j 5.d 6.k 7.n 8.b 9.l 10.m 11.i 12.h 13.a 14.f

18 1.current issue 2.postage 3.quotation 4.range 5.terms 6.following 7.note 8.reserve the right 9.accept delivery 10.acknowledge 11.line 12.regret 13.resume 14.inconvenience 15.supply 16.stock

19 1.compatible, data, program, software 2.closed shop, mediate, picket, strike 3.actuary, claim, policyholder, premium 4.dumping, embargo, export, tariff 5.bears, shares, speculate, stock exchange 6.judge, legal, sue, trial

20 1.accurate 2.retrieve 3.supplies 4.components 5.transactions 6.records 7.input 8.keyboard 9.floppy 10.modem 11.linked 12.output 13.screen 14.printer 15.single 16.continuous

21 1.make 2.do 3.make 4.make 5.do 6.doing 7.made 8.make 9.doing 10.made 11.do 12.make 13.make 14.make 15.do 16.done 17.made 18.done

22 1.j 2.k 3.k 4.a 5.h 6.i 7.c 8.g 9.e 10.f 11.l 12.d

23 1.set 2.issue 3.promised delivery 4.passed 5.deducted 6.matter 7.further delay 8.reply 9.refund 10.obliged 11.regret the delay 12.despatching 13.dealing 14.mislaid 15.apologise for 16.deter

24 1.b 2.b 3.b 4.c 5.d 6.a 7.b 8.a 9.c 10.c 11.a 12.c 13.b 14.c 15.c 16.b

25 1.sold 2.taken over 3.made 4.said 5.overcome 6.built 7.won 8.spent 9.sent 10.told 11.known 12.held 13.underwritten 14.lost 15.set up 16.stolen

26 1.Board 2.Managing 3.Accountant 4.Administration 5.Manager 6.Personnel 7.Head 8.Salaries 9.Stock 10.Mail 11.Processing 12.Market 13.Advertising 14.Control 15.Recruitment 16.Innovation

27 A 1.pointer 2.overhead projector 3.slide projector 4.handout 5.felt tip pen 6.screen 7.pie chart 8.graph 9.bar chart 10.podium 11.notes 12.microphone 13.curtain 14.flip chart
   B 1.May I begin 2.at such short notice 3.As you know 4.purpose 5.up to date 6.First of all 7.Next 8.Finally 9.priorities 10.draw your attention 11.As far as 12.as a whole 13.On the contrary 14.On the other hand 15.In other words 16.to sum up

28 Set 1 1.e 2.b 3.g 4.c 5.h 6.d 7.f 8.a Set 2 1.e 2.b 3.f 4.h 5.g 6.a 7.c 8.d 1.reduce costs 2.arrange a demonstration 3.settle disputes 4.build a factory

29 1.conveniently 2.satisfactorily 3.widely 4.fully 5.financially 6.specially 7.eventually 8.absolutely 9.strictly 10.considerably 11.correctly 12.temporarily 13.virtually 14.tactfully 15.favourably 16.actively

30 1.b 2.c 3.a 4.d 5.a 6.c 7.a 8.b 9.a 10.b 11.c 12.a 13.d 14.c 15.c

31 1.complimentary copy 2.recent publications 3.highly popular 4.extensively trialled 5.favourable response 6.suitable 7.recommend 8.experience 9.needs 10.featured 11.terms of payment 12.further information 13.representatives 14.specially selected 15.value 16.confident 17.colleagues 18.subscription form 19.convenience 20.eligible

32 Set 1 1.g 2.e 3.b 4.f 5.c 6.a 7.d 8.h Set 2 1.b 2.a 3.e 4.g 5.h 6.d 7.f 8.c 1.mouth-watering recipes 2.highly-trained staff 3.perfect fit 4.stress-free driving

33 1.rejected 2.demolishing 3.attacked 4.withdraw 5.accept 6.succeed 7.imposed 8.gained 9.lost 10.keep 11.lower 12.increase 13.complicate 14.strengthen 15.expanded 16.agreed

34 1.unemployment, employee, employer, employment 2.engaged, engagements 3.expensive, expenses, expenditure, expense 4.explanatory, explanation 5.extended, extension, extensively, extent 6.financial, financially 7.growing, growth 8.impression, impressive, unimpressed 9.industrial, industrialist, industrialised/ized 10.inflated, inflation, inflationary 11.information, informative, misinformed 12.instructions, instruction 13.introductory, introduction 14.investment, investors 15.knowledge, unknown, knowledgeable 16.illegal, legality

35 1.purchase (buy) 2.perceive (see) 3.elapsed (passed) 4.facilitate (make easier) 5.require (need) 6.terminate (end) 7.anticipate (expect) 8.undertaken (promised, agreed) 9.comprehend (understand)

36 1.b 2.d 3.a 4.b 5.b 6.a 7.d 8.a 9.c 10.d 11.c 12.d 13.a 14.a

37 1.d 2.g 3.k 4.j 5.l 6.a 7.i 8.b 9.e 10.h 11.c 12.f

38 A 1.kitchen staff 2.outgoing 3.hard work 4.suit 5.contact 6.required 7.busy office 8.preference 9.willing 10.initiative 11.clear 12.thorough training 13.potential customers 14.successful candidate 15.experience 16.skills 17.ability 18.team 19.attractive 20.pension scheme B 1.to 2.in 3.position 4.further 5.form 6.for 7.enclose 8.as 9.audio 10.with 11.enquiries 12.take 13.opportunity 14.available 15.consider 16.favourably

39 1.ran out 2.carried out 3.set up 4.stood in 5.came out 6.stopped over/off 7.drew up 8.brought ... forward 9.relied on 10.gave in 11.left out 12.laid off 13.stuck to 14.paid back

40 1.a 2.b 3.b 4.c 5.b 6.a 7.b 8.b 9.b 10.d 11.a 12.d 13.b 14.a 15.c

41 1.confident 2.relevant 3.efficient 4.insolvent 5.permanent 6.significant 7.redundant 8.convenient 9.constant 10.current 11.dominant 12.consistent 13.extravagant 14.reluctant 15.dependent

42 Set 1 1.h 2.f 3.b 4.d 5.e 6.g 7.c 8.a Set 2 1.h 2.a 3.b 4.f 5.c 6.g 7.d 8.e 1.alternative arrangements 2.multi-national company 3.potential customer 4.close attention

43 1.a 2.c 3.d 4.a 5.c 6.b 7.a 8.c 9.c 10.a 11.c 12.b 13.c 14.c 15.d

44 1.date stamp 2.guillotine 3.note pad 4.paper clips 5.pencil sharpener 6.punch 7.ruler 8.scales 9.scissors 10.stamps 11.stapler 12.staples 13.string 14.tray 15.wastepaper bin 16.calculator

45 1.admiration for 2.effect on 3.access to 4.confidence in 5.solution to 6.interest in 7.chance of 8.emphasis on 9.experience of 10.point in 11.increase in 12.intention of 13.congratulations on 14.result of

46 1.g 2.i 3.n 4.c 5.k 6.p 7.j 8.o 9.d 10.l 11.e 12.b 13.f 14.m 15.h 16.a 1.productivity bonus 2.assembly line 3.takeover bid 4.market research 5.salary scale 6.balance sheet

47 1.R&D Manager 2.personnel officer 3.draughtsperson 4.clerk 5.assembly person 6.salesperson 7.accountant 8.chauffeur 9.motor mechanic 10.receptionist 11.computer operator 12.advertising executive 1.existing range 2.essential member 3.nightshift 4.pragmatic approach 5.clean driving licence 6.particular responsibilities

48 1.b 2.b 3.c 4.b 5.b 6.b 7.a 8.c 9.b 10.d 11.d 12.a 13.a 14.b

49 1.take out 2.take on 3.taken ... consideration 4.took off 5.take home 6.take ... call 7.take steps 8.take ... chair 9.take ... seriously 10.take ... down 11.taken over 12.take ... further 13.take charge 14.taking ... risk 15.take up

50 1.woo 2.teething problems 3.thorny problem 4.ride rough-shod 5.undermine 6.on the grapevine 7.carry the can 8.ride the storm 9.hefty knock 10.wiped off 11.type-cast 12.rubber-stamp 13.fall by the wayside 14.a dawn raid 15.nose-dive

51 1.advice 2.briefly 3.seat 4.check 5.compliments 6.conform 7.confidential 8.conscientious 9.economic 10.rebate 11.fee 12.income 13.industrial 14.mislaid 15.notes 16.takeover 17.price 18.productivity

52 1.management, Managing, manageable 2.negotiable, negotiations 3.unoccupied, occupational 4.operation, operating, operational, operator 5.optional, options 6.originally, originated, originality 7.preference, preferential 8.production, product, unproductive, productivity 9.unprofitable, profitably, profitability 10.restrictions, restrictive, restricted 11.satisfaction, satisfactory, dissatisfied 12.systematic, systematically 13.suitability, suitable 14.variety, variable, various

53 1.b 2.c 3.d 4.c 5.c 6.a 7.c 8.a 9.b 10.c 11.b 12.a 13.b 14.a 15.d

54 1.black 2.black 3.green 4.green 5.black ... white 6.white 7.red 8.red 9.grey 10.red 11.black 12.white 13.blue 14.red 15.green 16.black

55 1.familiar with 2.eligible for 3.available for 4.envious of 5.Contrary to 6.popular with 7.consistent with 8.responsible for 9.aware of 10.capable of 11.relevant to 12.accustomed to 13.acceptable to 14.dependent on 15.proud of 16.well-known for

56 Set 1 1.b 2.f 3.g 4.e 5.a 6.c 7.h 8.d Set 2 1.h 2.f 3.a 4.e 5.b 6.c 7.g 8.d 1.subsidise the staff canteen 2.pay duty 3.consult a lawyer 4.transfer funds

57 1.b 2.b 3.d 4.b 5.b 6.d 7.a 8.d 9.c 10.a 11.c 12.b 13.c 14.d 15.a 16.c 17.c 18.a 19.c 20.b 21.d 22.b 23.d 24.b 25.b 26.a 27.c 28.a

58 1.in a position to 2.in accordance with 3.in circulation 4.in debt 5.In round figures 6.in advance 7.in stock 8.in error 9.in due course 10.in the process of 11.in arrears 12.in transit

59 1.b 2.d 3.a 4.b 5.d 6.a 7.b 8.a 9.d 10.a 11.c 12.b 13.d 14.a

60 1.great pleasure 2.complimentary tickets 3.up to date 4.ideal opportunity 5.comprehensive range 6.new feature 7.series of lectures 8.speakers 9.emphasis 10.field 11.in-depth discussion 12.enclosed map 13.conveniently situated 14.enter 15.company details 16.look forward

61 1.contract 2.practice 3.convenience 4.absence 5.earnings 6.error 7.notice 8.embarkation 9.return 10.charges 11.hands 12.living 1.rate of return 2.flag of convenience 3.breach of contract 4.show of hands 5.code of practice

62 1.h 2.i 3.e 4.j 5.k 6.b 7.a 8.c 9.f 10.g 11.l 12.d

63 1.b 2.c 3.a 4.d 5.c 6.d 7.b 8.a 9.a 10.c 11.b 12.a 13.d 14.a 15.d

64 1.systematically 2.readily 3.wholly 4.consistently 5.formally 6.absolutely 7.firmly 8.convincingly 9.irretrievably 10.initially 11.adversely 12.instantaneously 13.highly 14.unpredictably

65 1.training sessions 2.suitable 3.requirements 4.single 5.provide 6.quotation 7.full board 8.brochure 9.meet 10.reasonable rates 11.available 12.urge 13.without delay 14.require 15.hesitate 16.pleasure

66 1.unnecessary paperwork 2.separate folders 3.members of staff 4.Set priorities 5.put off unpleasant tasks 6.lose concentration 7.Delegate routine tasks 8.time-consuming way 9.have a meeting 10.set a time limit 11.Skip over 12.pick out

67 1.b 2.c 3.d 4.c 5.a 6.b 7.c 8.b 9.c 10.a 11.d 12.b 13.c 14.b 15.a

Words included in Build Your Business Vocabulary

(The numbers refer to exercises.)

94